SCREENING TOOL FOR ENERGY EVALUATION OF PROJECTS

A REFERENCE GUIDE FOR ASSESSING WATER SUPPLY AND WASTEWATER TREATMENT SYSTEMS

APRIL 2021

ASIAN DEVELOPMENT BANK

ADB

CONTENTS

TABLES, FIGURES, AND BOX

ACKNOWLEDGMENTS

The Screening Tool for Energy Evaluation of Projects (STEEP) is designed to help improve energy use efficiency in new or existing water and wastewater treatment systems. This reference guide provides a comprehensive overview of the STEEP and was developed in a One-Asian Development Bank (ADB) spirit with the collaborative efforts of Stephane Bessadi (Senior Procurement Specialist, ADB), Rodney Chapin (Consultant and chief executive officer of Ardurra International), Alexandra Conroy (Urban Development Specialist, ADB), and Aldrin Plaza (Urban Development Officer, ADB). This reference guide also builds on the earlier work undertaken by ADB in collaboration with the International WaterCentre based in Brisbane, Australia

This reference guide is a joint endeavor of the Urban and Water Sector Groups of ADB with the strong support of Thomas Panella (Chief of Water Sector Group, ADB) and Manoj Sharma (Chief of Urban Sector Group, ADB), and their respective teams. Substantive review and guidance on the manuscript preparation was also provided by Robert Guild (Chief Sector Officer, ADB). Technical review and inputs were provided by Luca Di Mario (Urban Development Specialist, ADB), David Elzinga (Senior Energy Specialist, ADB), Cesar Llorens (Senior Urban Development Specialist, ADB), Dan Millison (Consultant, ADB), and Yongping Zhai (Chief of Energy Sector Group, ADB).

Special thanks go to the ADB operations teams who supported the pilot and ongoing project activities using the tool, as well as to Rustam Adbukayumov (Procurement Division 2 Director, ADB) who also supported this work.

Administrative and editorial support to the manuscript were provided by Lindy Lois Gamolo, Karen Lapitan, Gino Pascua, and Elyn Ruth Ravancho from the Urban Sector Group Secretariat. High appreciation is also expressed for the guidance and support provided by the team from ADB's Department of Communications, composed of Rodel Bautista, Cynthia Hidalgo, April Gallega, and Anthony Victoria.

The publication was edited by Ma. Josefa Gonzalez, typeset by Joe Mark Ganaban, and page-proof checked by Ma. Cecilia Abellar.

ABBREVIATIONS

ADB	–	Asian Development Bank
CO_2	–	carbon dioxide
DMC	–	developing member country
GHG	–	greenhouse gas
KPI	–	key performance indicator
kWh	–	kilowatt-hour
m^3	–	cubic meter
NRW	–	nonrevenue water
STEEP	–	Screening Tool for Energy Evaluation of Projects

1 INTRODUCTION

1.1 Screening Tool for Energy Evaluation of Projects Explained

Water supply and wastewater treatment services are basic but critical utilities that have major roles in supporting social and domestic needs of people, sustaining local economic activities, and ensuring healthy urban environments. By 2050, about 65% of the population in Asia and the Pacific are expected to live in cities. This dictates the need to increase access to water supply and wastewater management services. The increase in service coverage would also translate to additional investments by water utility operators, which will lead to increased energy demand in their operations. This means energy management should be incorporated into the designs of urban water supply and wastewater utility investments to ensure optimal operations.

The Asian Development Bank (ADB) has an extensive portfolio of water supply and wastewater investment projects in its developing member countries (DMCs) in Asia and the Pacific, and the number of these projects has steadily increased annually since 2010. Out of ADB's average annual investments of about $2 billion under the water and other urban infrastructure services projects, 40%–60% are on water supply and wastewater investment projects. These investments focused primarily on the quantity (supply, nonrevenue water, etc.), duration (continuous service), and quality (water quality, health, etc.) of service to improve livability conditions of communities in cities and towns in the region. However, due to rapid urbanization, statistics showed that countries in Asia and the Pacific generate approximately 40% of the world's greenhouse gas (GHG) emissions.[1] It should be noted that this incidence is determined without yet any consideration on the energy use or possible GHG emissions from water supply and wastewater system facilities.

A number of computer-based tools have been developed to support energy assessments, such as Sigma software and AWARE-P. These are also designed to support the International Water Association's Performance Indicators for Water Supply Services.

Given its decades of experience in designing and implementing water supply and wastewater management projects, ADB has also embarked on developing a computer-based tool for energy evaluation of urban water supply and wastewater management projects called the Screening Tool for Energy Evaluation of Projects (STEEP).

STEEP is a free Excel-based reference guide that can be used to make system assessments and identify potential areas for energy use savings in existing or planned water supply and wastewater facility projects. Since 2017, STEEP has been continuously developed based on lessons and experiences from pilot assessments carried out in various water and wastewater investment projects financed by ADB.[2]

---

[1] ADB. 2016. *The Asian Development Bank and the Climate Investment Funds Country Fact Sheets*. Manila.
[2] To view the STEEP and the detailed instructions on how to use it, visit ADB's Vision of Livable Cities. Toolkits: Screening Tool for Energy Evaluation of Projects (STEEP). https://www.livablecities.info/steep.

Based on the results of pilot assessments and accepted principles of energy management, the potential energy savings can range from 20% to 80%, depending on the type and stage of project implementation. Table 1 presents the range of savings and possible sources in water supply production and wastewater treatment system facilities based on the pilot assessment conducted.

Table 1: Possible Sources and Range of Savings in a Water Supply and Wastewater Treatment System

System Source for Potential Savings	Range of Savings
Operations	5%–30%
Mechanical systems	5%–20%
Process	5%–30%
Electrical systems	5%–20%
Use of advanced technology	10%–30%
Use of smart management systems	10%–25%
Reduction of physical losses	5%–50%

Source: Asian Development Bank.

Importance of Energy Screening

Energy Utilization in Water Utility Operations

Energy use, or simply consumption, occurs at many points within the domestic water cycle (Figure 1). Accepted benchmarks indicate that the average energy intensity (specific energy use) for water extraction, treatment and distribution, and wastewater collection and treatment typically range from 0.5 to 0.6 kilowatt-hour per cubic meter (kWh/m^3). It is worth noting, however, that the energy intensity for specific systems varies depending on different factors. For water supply systems, these may include water source type, physical terrain of the facilities' location, and water quality parameters. For wastewater management systems, the factors affecting energy intensity include environmental discharge requirements, type of treatment, bioresources management, and physical terrain of the facilities' location.

Figure 1: Water and Wastewater System Energy Utilization

Wastewater
0.54 kWh/m³
Collection, treatment, and disposal

Potable Water Supply
0.52 kWh/m³
Transport, treatment, and distribution

kWh = kilowatt-hour, m³ = cubic meter.
Source: K. Bijl, ed. 2015. *Innovative Energy Recovery Strategies in the Urban Water Cycle.* Final Report Innovative Energy Recoveries Strategy (INNERS) Project. Zwolle.

Lessons and Experiences from STEEP's Pilot Activities

Under the guidance and leadership of ADB's Urban and Water Sector Groups, STEEP is continuously being improved since the initial pilot assessment in 2017. ADB's Pacific Department was the first to run a pilot test of the tool's applications and assess potential system energy savings in their water supply and wastewater treatment projects. The results showed potential energy savings (or energy production plus energy savings) ranging from 20% to over 50%, compared to the energy use or production of the existing system facilities. Follow-on system assessment exercises were also done for selected projects in ADB's Central and West Asia Department and East Asia Department.

The energy production associated with water and wastewater system facilities in ADB's DMCs were assessed in these pilots. Results showed that the total energy use of existing water and wastewater systems exceed 90 billion kilowatt-hours (kWh), and more than 64 million tons of carbon dioxide (CO_2) are produced annually. The recorded CO_2 is approximately 1% of all global emissions. This amount of annual emissions is expected to go up significantly as the water and wastewater coverage in the countries improve and will then increase to more than 2% of the total emissions generated. Section 4 provides details of these pilot activities.

Assuming that all of the existing water and wastewater system facilities in the DMCs are within this range of inefficiency (i.e., 40% as average), implementing the recommendations from STEEP could potentially save as much as 36 billion kWh of energy or more than 25 million tons of CO_2 emissions per year. At a conservative average electricity cost of $0.07 per kWh, the total savings annually for the utilities would exceed $2.5 billion. This would result to almost 0.5% savings of the total CO_2 emissions from these countries and could potentially double as the coverage ratio for water supply and wastewater systems reaches 100% in the region's DMCs.

It should be noted, however, that these projected impacts are only for direct energy use (electricity or fuel use). STEEP also includes a menu of best practices that can help improve and reduce the secondary energy use of systems without any compromise to the quantity, duration, or quality of the water supply, or wastewater management services provided.

With the rising energy demand and the need for sound climate mitigation action, it is important to promote and adopt water supply and wastewater management systems that operate with low energy use and with minimal GHG emissions. New technological and innovative tools have allowed water supply and wastewater service targets to be met with much less energy use. In some cases, these tools have adopted and utilized circular economy concepts to introduce energy production components as part of the system process. Energy efficiency, therefore, should now be considered a crucial factor in making considerations for system components that will be part of a design for water supply and wastewater management investment projects.

Overall, ADB's support and investments on water supply and wastewater management development, the immediate call to action to address the vulnerability to climate change, and the energy efficiency advances in water and wastewater technologies have driven the development of STEEP.

Benefits of Using STEEP

STEEP is intended to be a simple, practical, and flexible tool for ADB staff, consultants, and water utility managers. The tool can help the target users in developing and strengthening the climate mitigation components of an urban water supply and wastewater management investment project design.

STEEP offers a user-friendly interface for conducting a rapid assessment of system energy use. It has programmed assessment calculation tools and a menu of key performance indicators (KPIs), benchmarks, and best practices. The need to mainstream energy use in the design of water supply and wastewater management systems is becoming an imperative. The question now is how to effectively assess energy use and generate the information needed to make project design decisions based on the results of the assessment.

The said need has driven the development of STEEP, which aims to address two key concerns in water supply and wastewater management project design:

(i)   the need to improve the expertise and knowledge of ADB project officers in energy management in the water supply and wastewater management sector; and

(ii) the need to meet the basic service needs and demands, while considering system energy efficiency management measures and practices.

It has only been recently that both the advances in systems and the concern over energy efficiency and cost savings have gained attention for the development of such efficiency management measures. In addition, energy use within water supply and wastewater management system facilities can be a significant portion of the overall operating costs. In some systems, energy use can account for more than 50% of utility operations costs (WaterWorld, 2012).

Target Users of STEEP

ADB staff and consultants engaged by ADB are the intended users of STEEP. STEEP is a tool for undertaking technical due diligence at the project processing stage to assess the potential energy use and carbon footprint of water supply and/or wastewater infrastructure proposed under ADB's investment projects. Even nontechnical staff can benefit from using STEEP to produce a rapid assessment of actual or predicted energy use. ADB project officers can work with the borrowers technical team to reassess the proposed utility system design through more detailed assessments of a project's system components and technologies. Assessment outputs of STEEP will also contribute to preparing a strategic procurement plan for a project by providing analysis on the most energy-efficient options, as well as new technologies for review by borrowers. This will further help ensure greater energy efficiency and reduced carbon footprint at a larger scale through replication of such approaches in the design of subsequent investment projects in the energy, urban and water sectors.

Figure 2 proposes how the energy screening approach could be implemented in ADB project preparation.

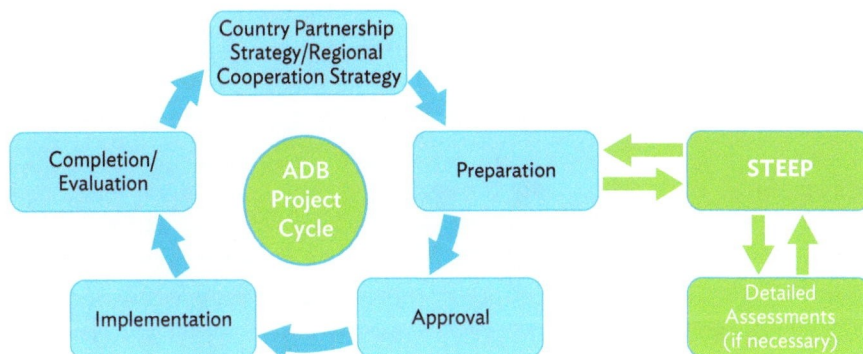

Figure 2: Entry Point for Application of the Screening Tool for Energy Evaluation of Projects in the ADB Project Cycle

ADB = Asian Development Bank, STEEP = Screening Tool for Energy Evaluation of Projects.
Source: ADB.

2 THE STEEP EVALUATION SYSTEM

Scope of Water and Wastewater Utility Energy Evaluation Using STEEP

Besides performing a rapid assessment of energy use for a proposed project vis-a-vis the baseline conditions of the existing water supply or wastewater management facilities, STEEP also compares the potential energy use of an ensuing investment project against a menu of benchmark norms and best practices. Thus, the output of the assessment does not only include the direct comparison to the baseline, but also provides guidance as to whether or not the proposed project's system design is within the limits of international benchmarks and adheres to best practices. STEEP also provides guidance in identifying the cause or areas of excessive energy use. This provides direction to the utility manager as to where to focus the technical improvements before conducting a detailed analysis on how to implement improvements.

STEEP evaluates baseline data (pre-project period) as compared to the forecast situation after the implementation of a proposed project or projects (post-project period). STEEP uses a Microsoft Excel interface and leads the user through a series of interfaces based on inputs and answers to select questions. The analysis through STEEP can be done with minimal required inputs and can be expanded by providing additional information.

STEEP is flexible and is designed to adjust to a specific project or system application. With this flexibility, it can be used to (i) assess the need for replacement or upgrading of an existing system (brownfield); (ii) guide the installation of a system, where one currently does not exist (greenfield); and (iii) compare existing systems to benchmarks and best practices, or simply to identify potential energy savings opportunities within a water supply and/or wastewater management system facilities.

In a **brownfield system,** STEEP can evaluate the existing system, particularly if a retrofit or upgrading is necessary. In general, some of the common inefficiencies found in brownfield systems are related to (i) deteriorated assets; (ii) outdated or inefficient electrical and mechanical systems; (iii) high nonrevenue water (NRW); (iv) lack of automation; and (v) inefficient wastewater treatment regimes (i.e., biological, chemical, and/or physical).

In a **greenfield system,** STEEP can help assess a proposed project's system design. For new projects, the frequent causes of energy inefficiencies, based on the pilot assessments, are (i) too much emphasis on the lowest capital cost, without optimization of operating costs; (ii) too much focus or redundancy included for continuous supply, such as overpumping, and lifting of excess supply to the highest pressure or storage; (iii) lack of consideration for energy reduction methods, such as zoning, smart systems, and electrical devices (e.g., variable frequency drives, capacitors, etc.); and (iv) lack of understanding on the future cost and impact of energy on systems.

Data Requirements

As an initial step in using STEEP, the user will key in a standard set of data to serve as inputs for STEEP to produce outputs using standard indicators for energy or resource use. STEEP is designed to operate on a minimum level of input data to provide baseline outputs. It is also capable of providing a more detailed assessment with additional data inputs. Overall, it takes 1 to 2 hours to input the data and generate the results. Some examples of required input data are the following:

(i)   period (number of days or months of data);
(ii)   service area population;
(iii) water production and use, or wastewater collected;
(iv)   number of connections within the system;
(v)   energy use (via electricity bills or fuel use); and
(vi)   minimal water quality parameters—e.g., for wastewater: five-day biochemical oxygen demand (BOD_5), chemical oxygen demand, etc.

The required data can be collected from operating records for the utility and may require field visits, based on the sophistication of the data and the record keeping practices of the utility management. A screenshot of the interface in the software tool showing a sample of required **inputs** for a water system assessment is presented in Table 2.

Table 2: Sample Water System Required Inputs

Rapid Assessment	Unit	Definition	Baseline Pre-Project Situation	Forecast Situation after Project Implementation	Comments
Number of Connections	connections	Number of connections to the distribution system and receiving the service, within the area of service managed by the utility.	5,000	9,000	
Population of Service Area	people	Number of inhabitants, within the area of service managed by the utility.	60,000	67,000	
Serviced (Connected) Population	people	Number of inhabitants, within the area of service managed by the utility, which are connected to the distribution system and are receiving the service.	22,000	67,000	
Total Water Produced[a]	m³	Total water consumed or used in the system, including (i) authorized consumption and (b) water loss.	740,000	1,800,000	
Authorized Consumption	m³	Sum of the volume of metered and nonmetered water that , during the assessment period, is taken by registered customers, water supplier, or others who are implicitly or explicitly authorized to do so by the water supplier, for residential, commercial, industrial, or public purposes (including water exported).	500,000	1,400,000	
Specific Carbon Production	kg CO_2/kWh	Specific CO_2 production per kWh for electricity generation mix in the service area.	0.50	0.50	If data are not available, use 0.50 kg CO_2/kWh.
Total Energy Consumed	kWh	Total energy consumed for the entire water supply utility, based on the utility bill during the assessment period.	150,000	400,000	

CO_2 = carbon dioxide, kg = kilogram, kWh = kilowatt-hour, m³ = cubic meter.
[a] Total water produced is equivalent to water input in the system including authorized consumption commercial and physical water losses.
Source: Asian Development Bank.

Data Processing and Analysis

From the inputs provided, STEEP will generate outputs in terms of KPIs, including additional outputs and graphical representations of the data. The KPIs are scored against the embedded menu of benchmarks and conventional norms in STEEP. This will provide the user with an indication of whether excess energy use is occurring or expected (via color-coded indicators discussed in section 2.4) and indications as to where within the system this may be occurring (depending on the level of input data).

Once the outputs are generated, the user can access the menu of benchmarks and best practices and determine why energy use may be excessive. STEEP will also provide recommendations on how to mitigate excess energy use. Based on the level of the energy use, the user and their technical team should be able to evaluate and devise solutions to address these energy inefficiencies.

Outputs of the Energy Evaluation Process through STEEP

The **outputs** generated by STEEP are categorized into three separate reports.

(i) **Scorecard.** STEEP generates a scorecard that provides relevant information, including KPIs. This scorecard provides the user with color-coded indicators for the key outputs considered: green (desirable), light green (at a range between desirable and marginal), yellow (marginal), orange (at a range between marginal and undesirable), and red (undesirable). This helps the user to determine immediately whether the energy use and other KPIs are within the acceptable norms or need further analysis. The scorecard also displays an *energy-water trajectory graph*, which indicates if the water use and energy use of the system is increasing on a unit basis (i.e., for upgrades to existing systems). Table 3 presents how a sample KPI output appears in the software tool's interface. The colors are data-driven to depict level of outputs from desirable to undesirable.

Table 3: Sample of Key Performance Indicators Generated

Parameter	Baseline Project Situation	Forecast Situation after Project Implementation	Unit	KPI Parameters
Energy Cost Ratio (energy cost/operating cost)	42.25	83.39	%	<20 desirable; 35 marginal; >50 undesirable
Energy Use per Authorized Consumption	0.30	2.90	kWh/m³	<0.45 desirable; 0.70 marginal; >1.30 undesirable
Energy Use per Produced Flow	0.19	2.18	kWh/m³	<0.35 desirable; 0.45 marginal; >0.65 undesirable
Nonrevenue Water	35.31	24.85	%	<20 desirable; 35 marginal; >50 undesirable
Per Capita Consumption (daily)	91.59	75.99	L/c/d	<100 desirable; 150 marginal; >250 undesirable
CO_2 Emissions per Capita (service area)	1.20	30.18	kg CO_2/c/year	<5 desirable; 10 marginal; > 15 undesirable

c = capita, CO_2 = carbon dioxide, kg = kilogram, KPI = key performance indicator, kWh = kilowatt-hour, L/c/d = liters per capita per day, m³ = cubic meter.
Note: The colors in the table are data-driven to depict level of outputs: green (desirable), light green (at a range between desirable and marginal), yellow (marginal), orange (at a range between marginal and undesirable), and red (undesirable).
Source: Asian Development Bank.

(ii) **Supplemental outputs.** These outputs are additional calculations done through STEEP based on the level of input information provided by the user. This page generates relevant outputs with respect to the additional inputs provided. For example, if the user has access to electricity data from various metering sources within the system, those data can be used as input to provide a more detailed assessment of energy use for specific systems (e.g., pumping, treatment, etc.). This will help guide the user in identifying the particular source or sources of energy inefficiency within the system.

(iii) **Graphs.** STEEP also provides graphical representations of selected outputs for the user to have comparative information on the pre-project conditions vis-a-vis the baseline. The graphs are generated to help the user visualize the needed or proposed changes, as well as identify concerns associated with these changes in energy use.

3 OPPORTUNITIES FOR ENERGY SAVINGS IN WATER SUPPLY AND WASTEWATER TREATMENT UTILITIES

Results of the pilot assessments revealed that potential energy savings opportunities generally fall into a small set of categories. Table 4 provides a summary as to where the energy inefficiencies may most likely be found in a system, or the potential areas for generating energy savings in a water supply or wastewater treatment system. A more detailed description of the potential areas for energy savings or energy production in water supply systems (section 3.1) and wastewater management systems (section 3.2) follows.

Table 4: Opportunities for Energy Savings or Production

High Likelihood	High Impact
Water Supply Systems	
Nonrevenue water (technical losses)	Nonrevenue water (technical losses)
Overreliance on active methods (storage/pumping/pressure control) for pressure/supply	Overreliance on active methods (storage/pumping/pressure control) for pressure/supply
Operating plan not focused on energy savings	Inadequate/insufficient zoning
Lack of pressure management systems	Replacement of membrane filtration with low-pressure conventional filtration
	Production of hydropower energy from water source abstraction
Wastewater Treatment Systems	
Inefficient aeration systems (mechanical)	Inefficient aeration systems (mechanical)
Inadequate control of aeration system	Inadequate control of aeration system
Overreliance on oxic (aerated) systems and/or chemical treatment	Management of bioresources through low-energy methods
	Beneficial reuse of bioresources and/or nutrients

Source: Asian Development Bank.

Energy Savings Opportunities in Water Supply Systems

Energy use in a water supply system is heavily dependent on the volume of water pumped. The system's level of nonrevenue water (NRW) and operations management practices are crucial factors as well. On the average, more than 60% of the energy used in water supply systems comes from pumping systems (Bijl, 2015). Figure 3 shows a typical water system and the points of interest for both energy use and energy production.

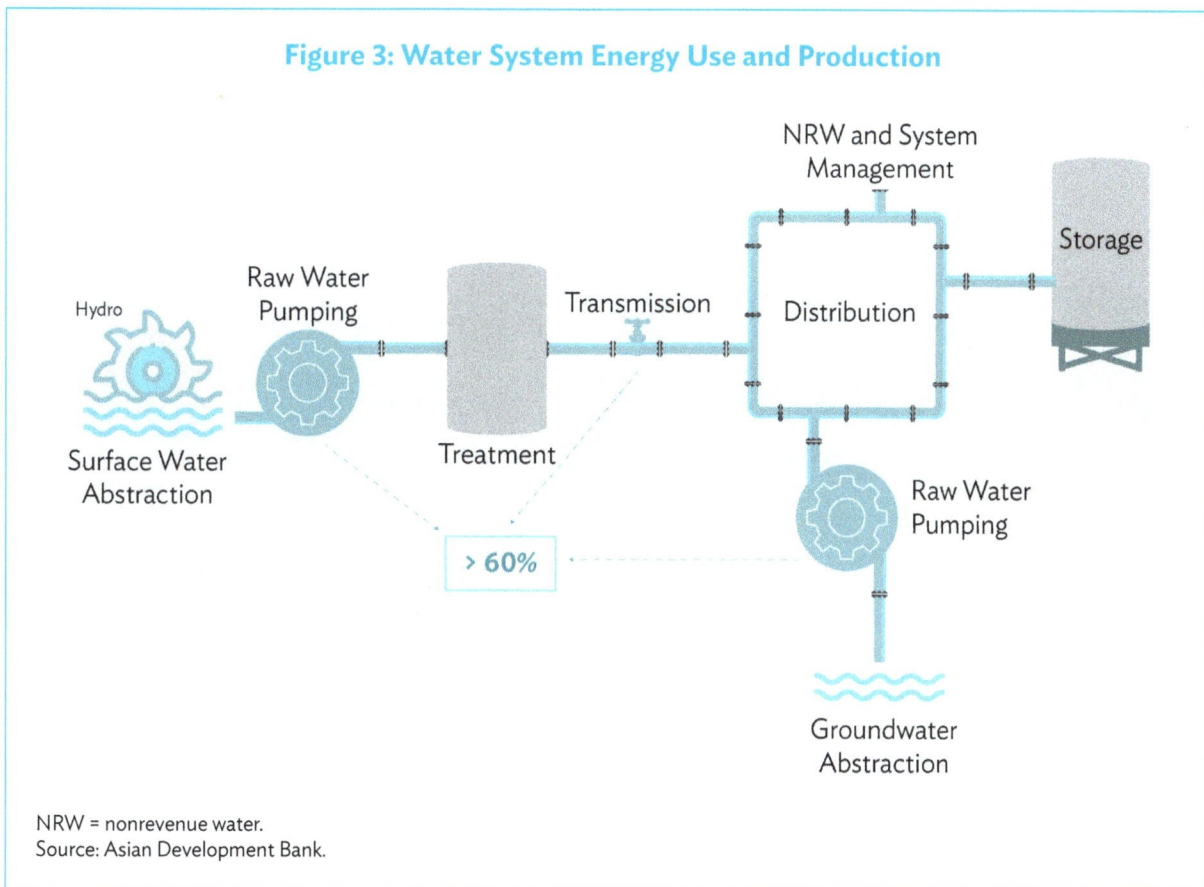

Figure 3: Water System Energy Use and Production

NRW = nonrevenue water.
Source: Asian Development Bank.

Water supply pumping systems are greatly affected by the facility's physical terrain, service area locations, pressure management, and NRW. Therefore, the challenge in energy use for water supply systems is to manage pressure within the system and reduce NRW to globally acceptable levels. For surface water, conventional treatment typically involves low pressure or gravity granular media filtration. Microfiltration and ultrafiltration membrane systems consume more energy, but offer more advantage in terms of their smaller footprint where land availability is a constraint. In cases where it is necessary to treat high salinity water or water containing low molecular weight compounds, membrane desalination may be warranted. However, compared to low pressure systems, this will result to higher energy consumption.

In terms of energy production, there are opportunities in having hydropower generation facilities between the extraction point and the treatment or distribution system. This can be done by capturing hydropower energy from water transmission pipes or canal transmission lines with the use of in-line hydropower generator technologies (Figure 4). An in-line hydropower generator can be used in points in water piping system where there is extra dynamic head that can be consumed and can be used to power activities such as system maintenance work or water system monitoring devices linked to central monitoring systems (Chen et al., 2013). This eliminates the necessity to draw electricity from the utility's power supply systems for such work. Another possibility of energy production in water supply systems is by installing floating solar panels in water supply reservoirs to augment energy requirements in the facility such as for perimeter and building lighting.

Figure 4: Series of In-Line Hydropower Generators

Source: J. Chen et al. 2013. A Novel Vertical Axis Water Turbine for Power Generation from Water Pipelines. *Energy*. 54. pp. 184–193.

Energy Savings Opportunities in Wastewater Management Systems

For wastewater management systems, the energy use and opportunities for energy production (or resources) are usually more complex. The single greatest consumer of energy within wastewater systems is typically secondary (biological) treatment systems through aeration. Figure 5 shows the energy use profile and areas for potential energy (or resource) production within wastewater systems.

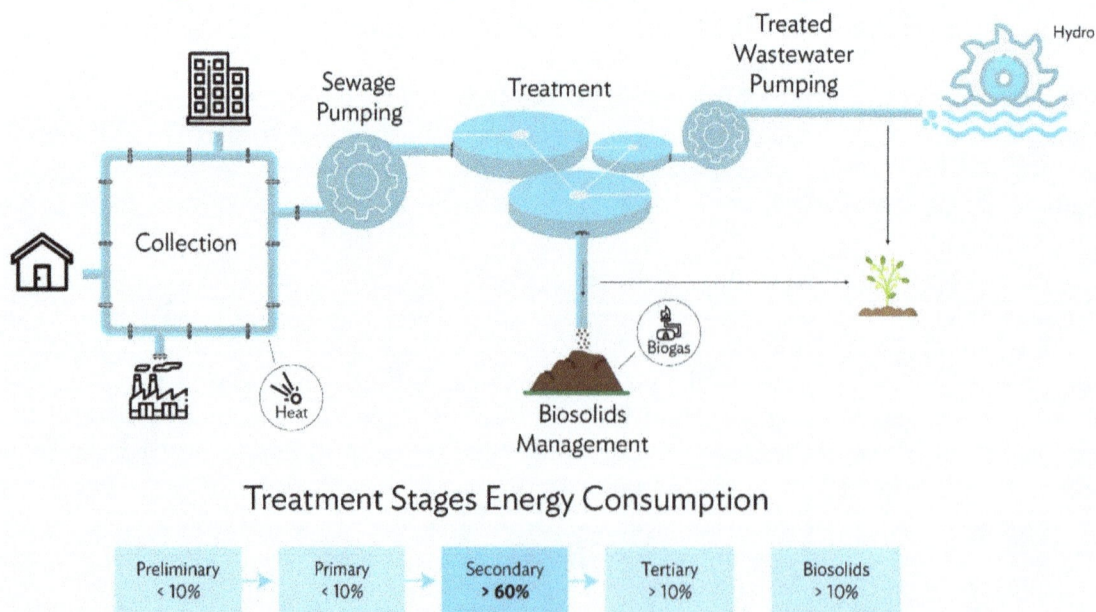

Figure 5: Wastewater System Energy Use and Energy Production

Note: Among the wastewater treatment stages, the greatest consumer of energy is the secondary (biological) treatment systems.
Source: Asian Development Bank.

Research has shown that more than 60% of the energy consumed in wastewater treatment occurs within secondary treatment systems (Bijl, 2015). However, there are now systems and technologies that can help reduce this energy use. Some systems are even capable of operating at energy neutral when considering both treatment and recovery of energy or resources. Figure 6 shows the potential energy that exists within wastewater management systems as compared to the energy needed for wastewater treatment.

Figure 6: Theoretical Energy Content of Wastewater versus Treatment Options

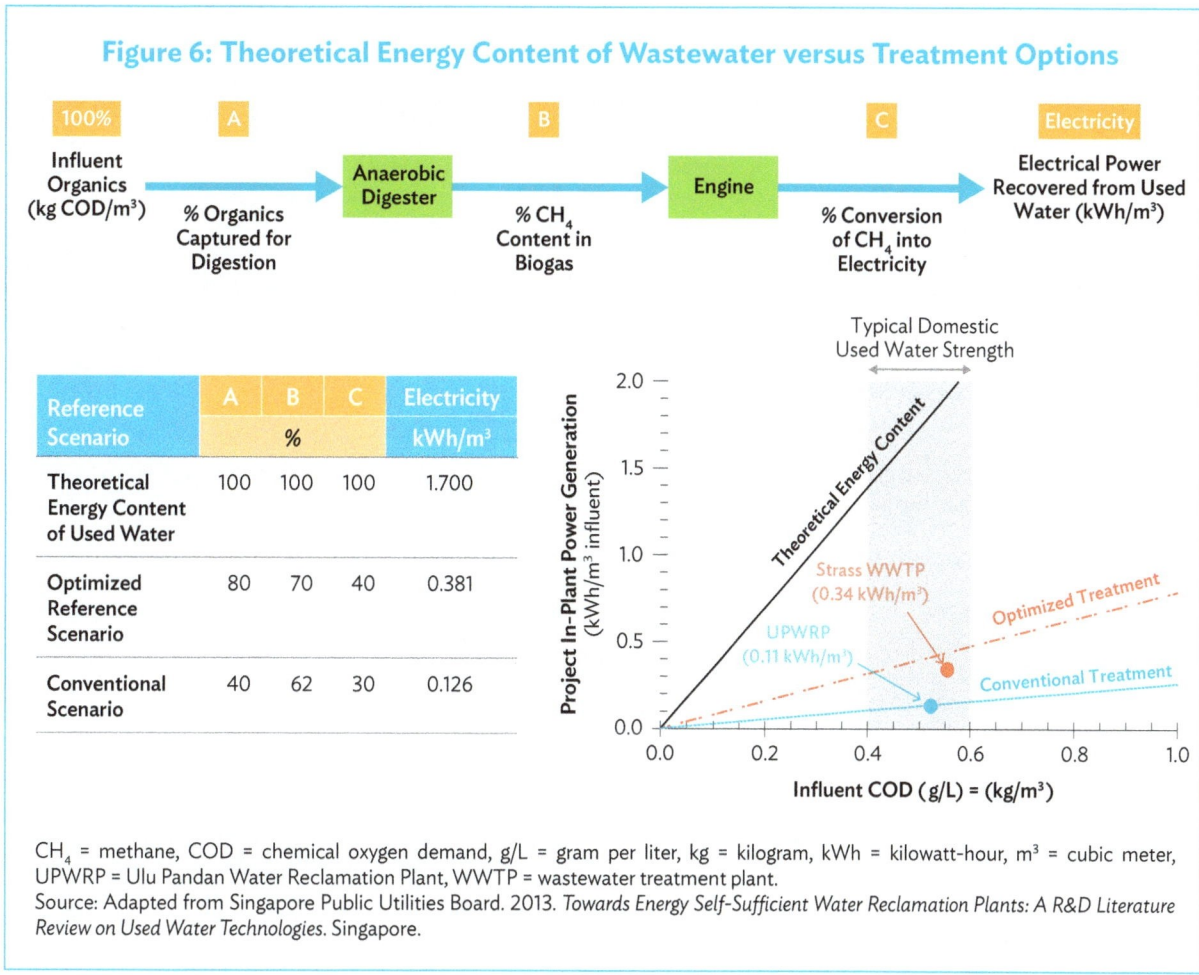

Reference Scenario	A	B	C	Electricity
	%			kWh/m³
Theoretical Energy Content of Used Water	100	100	100	1.700
Optimized Reference Scenario	80	70	40	0.381
Conventional Scenario	40	62	30	0.126

CH_4 = methane, COD = chemical oxygen demand, g/L = gram per liter, kg = kilogram, kWh = kilowatt-hour, m³ = cubic meter, UPWRP = Ulu Pandan Water Reclamation Plant, WWTP = wastewater treatment plant.
Source: Adapted from Singapore Public Utilities Board. 2013. *Towards Energy Self-Sufficient Water Reclamation Plants: A R&D Literature Review on Used Water Technologies.* Singapore.

Resource or energy production from wastewater management systems has already been practiced for many years, especially in advanced countries. Anaerobic digestion is the most common form of energy extraction from wastewater biosolids, where the process converts organics to methane (biogas), CO_2, and water while producing a stabilized product. In addition to anaerobic digestion, more advanced systems have been developed to hydrolyze, dry, or stabilize biosolids and produce resources (e.g., energy, organic soil amendments and/or fertilizers, etc.). In addition to extracting the energy from the organics in the wastewater through these methods, energy can also be extracted in the form of heat (for locations with winter seasons), while hydropower can be generated from wastewater treatment outfalls. For example, if there is a 1- to 2-meter elevation drop in treatment outfalls, low-head technologies such as Archimedes screw generators could be used. As with water supply reservoirs, another good example of energy recovery is by installing floating solar panels in wastewater lagoons. A combination of these measures can eventually be used as energy sources for wastewater facilities, which can lead to the possibility of making wastewater treatment systems in DMCs achieve a net-zero energy status in the future (the box presents a successful case of net-zero project).

Box: Achieving Net-Zero Energy Status for the Wastewater Treatment Plant Facility of Gresham City, Oregon State, United States

From 2005 to 2015, the city of Gresham, through thorough planning and implementation, was able to implement measures that enabled its wastewater treatment plant facility to achieve a net-zero energy status, with the plant now able to generate enough energy on-site to power its operations. The plant treats about 13 million gallons (or 50 million liters) of wastewater per day. The path toward achieving the plant's net-zero energy status was done in six phases over a 10-year period:

- **Phase 1:** Installation of 400-kilowatt (kW) co-generation engine with biogas scrubbing system;

- **Phase 2:** Installation of 420 kW solar energy system with 1,902 solar panels;

- **Phase 3:** Implementation of a power conservation project that reduced energy consumption in the whole plant by 14%;

- **Phase 4:** Installation of a 10,000-gallon fats, oil, and grease (FOG) receiving station from restaurants and food service establishments;

- **Phase 5:** Expansion of the FOG receiving station to 30,000 gallons; and

- **Phase 6:** Expansion of the co-generation system from 400 kW to 800 kW, doubling its biogas production for heating and electricity.

As a result of incorporating these clean energy technologies, the plant was able to save about $500,000 per year on electricity costs. In addition, the plant was also able to generate income of about $350,000 per year through fees for accepting FOG from regional food establishments, plus a number of awards, incentives, and tax credits from the government for the plant's contribution to carbon reduction efforts of the State of Oregon. The excess energy generated by the plant is sent out to the Portland General Electric grid, which is then distributed to families that receive energy assistance from the electric utility.

Source: G. Hayward. 2018. City of Gresham: Upgrading a Wastewater Treatment Plant to be Energy Net Zero. Center for Sustainable Infrastructure. Gresham, Oregon. August.

4 RESULTS FROM THE ASSESSMENT OF PILOT CASES ON USING STEEP

Pilot Case 1: Greenfield Desalination Example

The needs, constraints, costs, and other factors affecting energy utilization are magnified in remote countries like those in the Pacific. The next example was done for a Pacific DMC using desalination to augment existing water sources. While not resulting in any savings, this is a good example of how STEEP can be used to compare the forecast condition with benchmarks to assess the project.

Table 5, Table 6, and Figure 7 show the set of input data, process outputs, and scorecard of the project using STEEP's interface.[3]

Table 5: Input Data Set for the Desalination Plant Analysis

Rapid Assessment Input Data - Water Supply (Required Data Inputs Marked *)

Rapid Assessment	Units	Definitions	Baseline Pre-Project Situation	Forecast Situation after Project Implementation	Comments
Number of Connections*	connections	Number of connections to the distribution system and receiving the service, within the area of service managed by the utility	6,732	20,225	
Population of Service Area*	people	Number of inhabitants, within the area of service managed by the utility	130,062	145,473	
Serviced (Connected) Population*	people	Number of inhabitants, within the area of service managed by the utility, which are connected to the distribution system and are receiving the service	48,279	145,473	
Total Water Produced^a*	m^3	Total water consumed or used in the system, including (i) authorized consumption and (b) water loss	1,609,608	4,024,020	
Authorized Consumption*	m^3	Sum of the volume of metered and nonmetered water that , during the assessment period, is taken by registered customers, water supplier, or others who are implicitly or explicitly authorized to do so by the water supplier, for residential, commercial, industrial, or public purposes (includes water exported)	1,041,231	3,024,144	
Specific Carbon Production*	kg CO_2/kWh	Specific CO_2 production per kWh for electricity generation mix in the service area	0.50	0.50	If data are not available, use 0.50 kg CO_2/kWh.

continued on next page

---

[3] Input data provided in this case example are adjusted to ensure data de-identification.

Table 5 *continued*

Rapid Assessment	Units	Definitions	Baseline Pre-Project Situation	Forecast Situation after Project Implementation	Comments
Total Energy Consumed*	kWh	Total energy consumed for the entire water supply utility, based on the utility bill during the assessment period	311,060	8,780,794	
Residential Consumption	m³	Proportion of the authorized consumption which is supplied for residential purposes	804,518	2,759,385	
Residential Water Use Breakdown-Outdoor Use	m³	Proportion of the residential water consumption used outdoors (e.g., garden)	NA	NA	
Residential Water Use Breakdown-Showers/Bath	m³	Proportion of the residential water consumption used in showers and/or baths	120,679	1,241,724	
Residential Water Use Breakdown-Clothes Washing	m³	Proportion of the residential water consumption used in washing clothes	NA	689,845	
Residential Water Use Breakdown-Leakage	m³	Proportion of the residential water consumption lost due to leakage	536,345	919,796	
Residential Water Use Breakdown-Other Water Use	m³	Proportion of the residential water consumption used in other uses not mentioned above	NA	NA	
Industrial Consumption	m³	Proportion of authorized consumption supplied for industrial purposes	236,713	264,761	
Commercial Consumption	m³	Proportion of authorized consumption supplied for commercial purposes	NA	NA	
Other Public Consumption	m³	Proportion of authorized consumption which is supplied for other public purposes	32,032	80,080	
Average Tariff	$/m³	Average tariff for the authorized water consumption for all categories (residential, industrial, commercial, etc.)	NA	3.00	
Renewable Energy Consumed	kWh	Total renewable energy consumed during the assessment period	NA	NA	
Energy Costs	$	Cost from electricity consumption for the entire water supply utility, based on the utility bill during the assessment period	128,313	3,680,466	
Operating Costs	$	Total operation and maintenance net costs and internal human resources net costs (i.e., not including the capitalized cost of self-constructed assets) related to the water supply within the service area managed by the utility during the entire assessment	303,728	4,413,378	
Volume of Fuel Consumed	L	Fuel consumption in water supply, for instance, due to the use of on-site generators or devices that works on fuel (e.g., fuel engines for pumps)	NA	NA	
Abstraction — Energy Consumed	kWh	Electric energy consumption for water abstraction stage, by the utility during the entire assessment period	103,884	746,403	
Abstraction — Energy Cost	$	Electric energy cost for water abstraction stage, by the utility during the entire assessment period	NA	NA	
Abstraction — Volume of Conveyed Water	m³	Sum of the water abstracted (gravity or pumped) in the abstraction stage, by the utility during the entire assessment period	1,609,608	7,412,409	

continued on next page

Table 5 *continued*

	Rapid Assessment	Units	Definitions	Baseline Pre-Project Situation	Forecast Situation after Project Implementation	Comments
Treatment	Electric Energy Produced from Turbines	kWh	Sum of the energy recovered during the assessment period by all turbines for abstracted water manage by the utility	NA	NA	
	Energy Consumed by Water Treatment Plants	kWh	Energy consumed during the assessment period by all urban water treatments plant managed by the utility	42,282	7,2017,180	
	Energy Cost of Water Treatment Plants	$	Energy cost during the assessment period by all urban water treatments plant managed by the utility	NA	NA	
	Energy Consumed by the Membrane Treatment Process (Membrane Only)	kWh	Energy consumed during the assessment period the membrane process for all water treatments plant managed by the utility	NA	6,569,314	
	Energy Cost of Membrane Treatment Process	$	Energy cost during the assessment period the membrane process for all water treatments plant managed by the utility	NA	NA	
	Volume of Water Treated	m³	Sum of the volume of water treated by the water treatment stage during the assessment period	1,609,608	7,412,409	
	Produced Water (Recovered Water)	m³	Some of the volume of water produced by the water treatment stage during the assessment period (minus reject water or water used for process)	1,609,608	4,024,020	
	Flux Rate (Membranes Only)	L/m²/hr	Unit treatment rate of the membranes (low pressure or RO)	NA	14	
	Membrane Operating Pressure (Membranes Only)	bar	Operating pressure of the membrane (low pressure or RO) operating within the water treatment plants	NA	51	
	Average Water Temperature (Membrane Only)	°C	Average yearly water temperature being treated through the membrane process	NA	28	
Distribution	Energy Consumed from the Grid	kWh	Energy consumed during the assessment period for the distribution system managed by the utility	164,894	786,249	
	Input Volume of Water	m³	Water volume entering the distribution system from the water treatment and/or directly from the abstraction during the assessment period	1,609,608	4,024,020	
	Authorized Consumption	m³	Sum of the volume metered and nonmetered water that during the assessment period is taken by registered customers, water supplier, or others who are implicitly or explicitly authorized to do so by the water supplier, for residential, commercial, industrial, or public purposes (includes water exported)	1,073,263	3,104,224	

$ = United States dollar, CO_2 = carbon dioxide, hr = hour, kg = kilogram, kWh = kilowatt-hour, L = liter, m² = square meter, m³ = cubic meter, NA = not applicable, RO = reverse osmosis.
[a] Total water produced is equivalent to water input in the system including authorized consumption commercial and physical water losses.
Source: Asian Development Bank.

Table 6: Desalination Plant Analysis Outputs

Parameter	Baseline Pre-Project Situation	Forecast Situation after Project Implementation	Unit
Energy Cost per Authorized Consumption	0.12	1.22	$/m³
Energy Cost per Produced Flow	0.08	0.91	$/m³
Energy Cost to Revenue (energy cost/revenue)	...	40.57	%
Energy Costs	128,313	3,680,466	$
Energy Use per Authorized Consumption	0.30	2.90	kWh/m³
Non-Energy Related Operating Costs	175,415	732,912	$
Nonresidential Consumption	236,713	264,759	m³
Nonrevenue Water	568,377	999,876	m³
Per Capita Connections	7.17	7.19	person/connection
Per Capita Energy Use	0.02	0.17	kWh/c/d
Per Capita Production	0.09	0.08	m³/c/d
Residential Consumption	804,518	2,759,385	m³
Total Operating Cost per Authorized Consumption	0.29	1.46	$/m³
Total Operating Cost per Produced Flow	0.19	1.10	$/m³
Water Supply Coverage	37.12	100.00	%
Working Ratio (operating cost/revenue)	...	48.65	%
Energy Cost Ratio (energy cost/operating cost)	42.25	83.39	%

... = data not available, $ = United States dollar, c = capita, d = day, kWh = kilowatt-hour, m³ = cubic meter.
Source: Asian Development Bank.

Figure 7: Desalination Plant Analysis Scorecard

Parameter	Baseline Project Situation	Forecast Situation after Project Implementation	Unit	KPI Parameters
Energy Use per Authorized Consumption	0.30	2.90	%	<0.45 desirable; 0.70 marginal; >1.30 undesirable
Energy Use per Produced Flow	0.19	2.18	kWh/m³	<0.35 desirable; 0.45 marginal; >0.65 undesirable
Nonrevenue Water	35.31	24.85	%	<20 desirable; 35 marginal; >50 undesirable
Per Capita Consumption (daily)	91.59	75.99	L/c/d	<100 desirable; 150 marginal; >250 undesirable

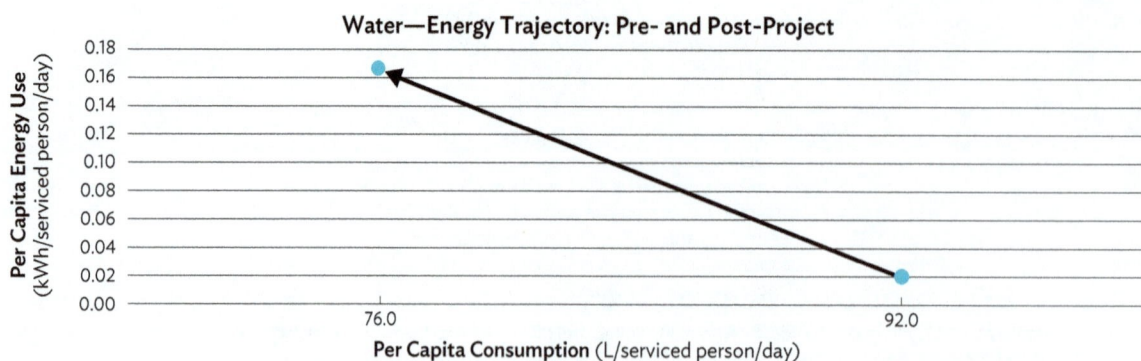

Water—Energy Trajectory: Pre- and Post-Project

KPI = key performance indicator, kWh = kilowatt-hour, L = liter, L/c/d = liters per capita per day, m³ = cubic meter.
Note: The colors in the table are data-driven to depict level of outputs: green (desirable), light green (at a range between desirable and marginal), yellow (marginal), orange (at a range between marginal and undesirable), and red (undesirable).
Source: Asian Development Bank.

Results of the desalination system analysis done through STEEP revealed that the system's energy use, compared to its initial design, has significantly increased. Results of the assessment showed that the increase could be attributed to the following reasons: (i) the served population is continuously increasing; (ii) the level of service is also significantly increasing; and (iii) the main water source of the system is transitioning from freshwater to saltwater. However, the additional production from desalination, in turn, reduces reliance on other water sources, including those that may be vulnerable to the impacts of climate change.

Figure 8 shows the summary of the results of the assessment on energy use for the desalination project using STEEP's interface.

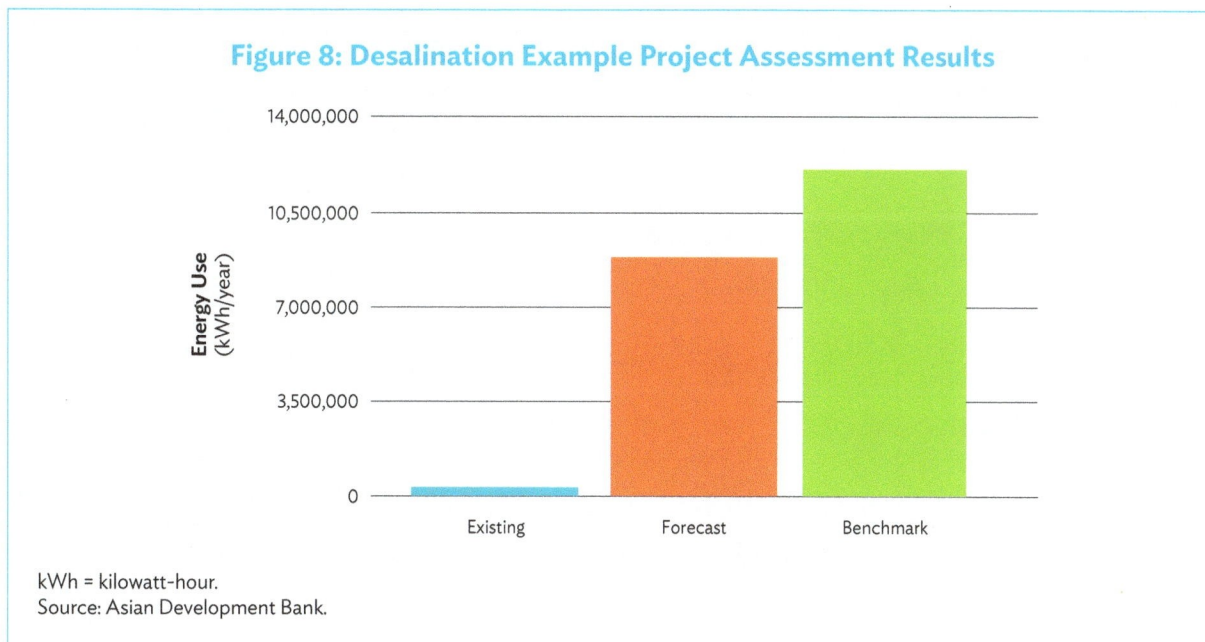

Figure 8: Desalination Example Project Assessment Results

kWh = kilowatt-hour.
Source: Asian Development Bank.

In this case, the benefit of using STEEP is that the utility manager could quickly ascertain that the design proposed by the technical team is below benchmark standards and in line with best practices. The water–energy trajectory graph also shows that the water supply system will be able operate more efficiently due to reduced network losses.

Figures 9–17 show some of the other analysis results comparing pre- and post-project conditions generated by STEEP.

Figure 9: Per Capita Consumption Analysis Output

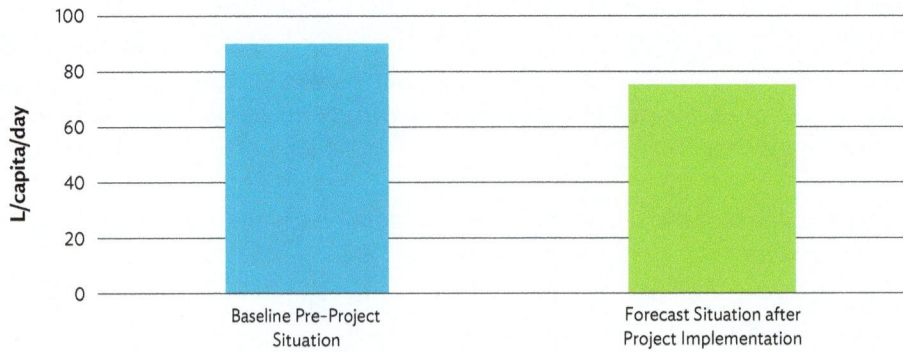

L = liter.
Source: Asian Development Bank.

Figure 10: Per Capita Energy Use Analysis Output

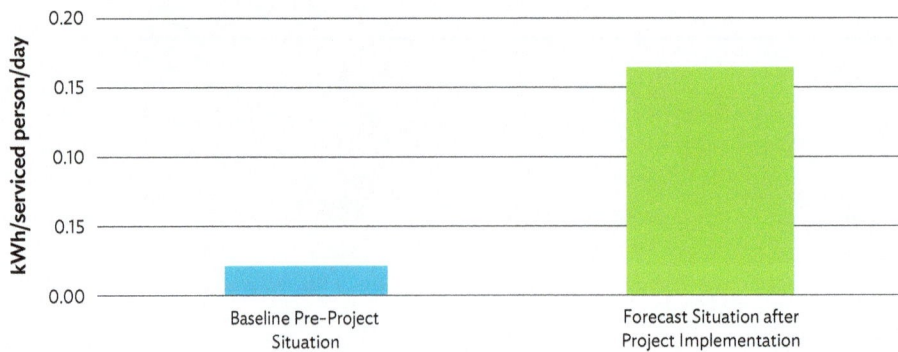

kWh = kilowatt-hour.
Source: Asian Development Bank.

Figure 11: Nonrevenue Water Analysis Output

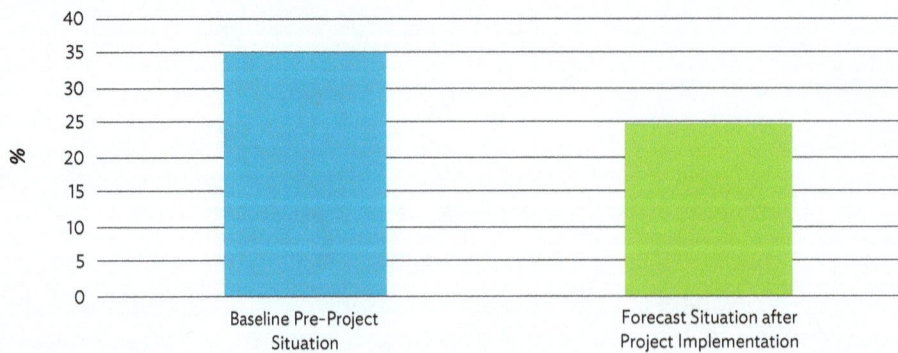

Source: Asian Development Bank.

Figure 12: Energy Use per Produced Flow Analysis Output

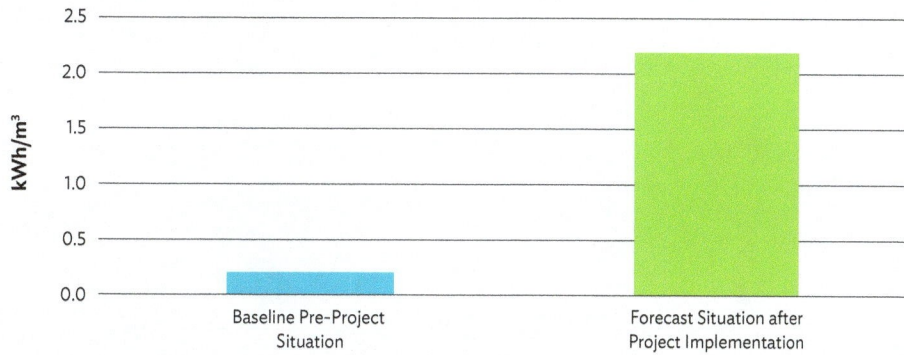

kWh = kilowatt-hour, m³ = cubic meter.
Source: Asian Development Bank.

Figure 13: Energy Use per Authorized Consumption Analysis Output

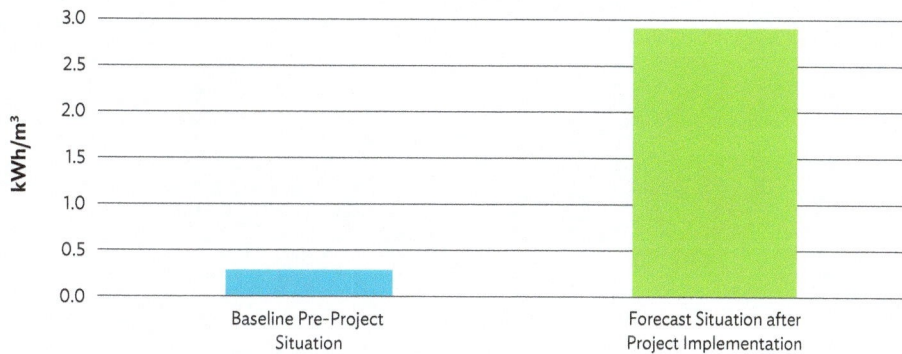

kWh = kilowatt-hour, m³ = cubic meter.
Source: Asian Development Bank.

Figure 14: Energy Cost to Revenue Analysis Output

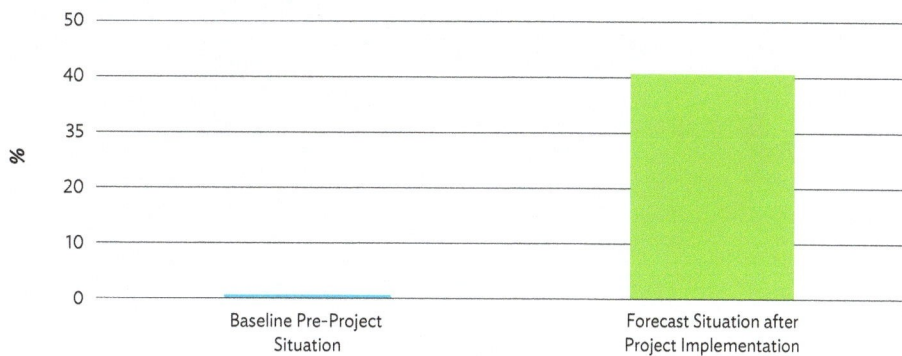

Source: Asian Development Bank.

Figure 15: Results of Authorized Consumption Analysis at Pre- and Post-Project

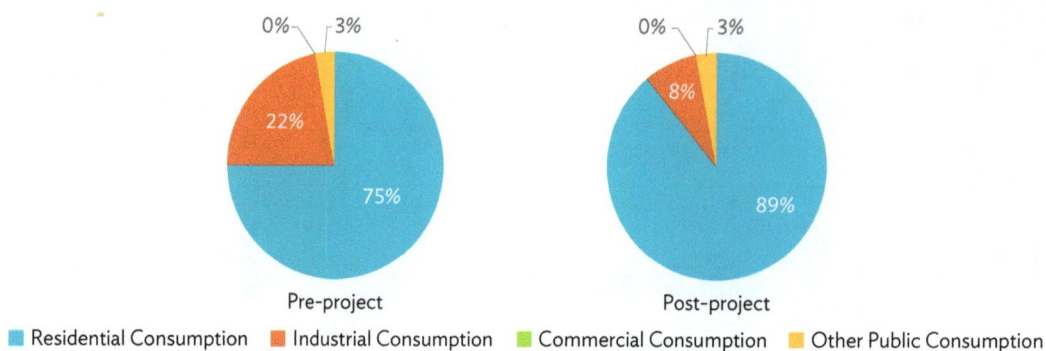

Pre-project

Post-project

■ Residential Consumption ■ Industrial Consumption ■ Commercial Consumption ■ Other Public Consumption

Source: Asian Development Bank.

Figure 16: Results of Operating Expenditure Cost Breakdown Analysis at Pre- and Post- Project

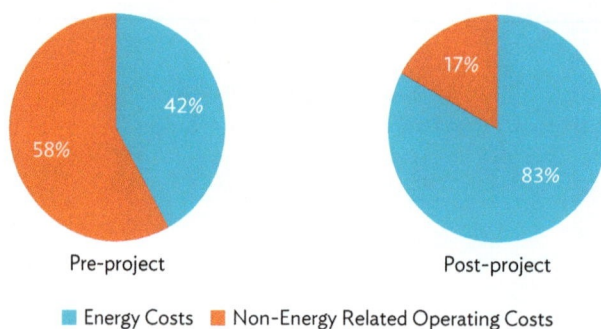

Pre-project

Post-project

■ Energy Costs ■ Non-Energy Related Operating Costs

Source: Asian Development Bank.

Figure 17: Results of Analysis on Annual Produced Water Supply at Pre- and Post-Project

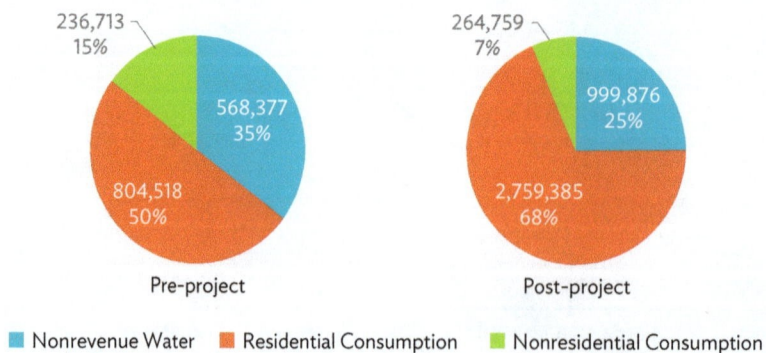

Pre-project

Post-project

■ Nonrevenue Water ■ Residential Consumption ■ Nonresidential Consumption

Note: Annual produced water expressed in cubic meters (m³).
Source: Asian Development Bank.

Pilot Case 2: Brownfield Water System Example

For this case, water supply systems from two separate cities were evaluated. In both cities, the energy efficiency assessment using STEEP was carried out when system facilities were being constructed. This case is an excellent example of the potential of STEEP as both cities could have been designed to provide the same level of service but with significantly more efficient energy use. Both Water System No. 1 and Water System No. 2 make use of groundwater as supply source and serving medium-sized cities.

■ Water System No. 1

Prior to the system upgrades, Water System No. 1 had a functioning water supply system, including both groundwater and surface water as sources. The system upgrades left both systems in place but increased the groundwater capacity to supply the entire system. This is because there are instances when the surface water supply cannot be used due to degrading water quality. Based on the operational plans and historic use, it was projected that the energy use would increase by approximately 20%–25% under the new scheme.

After a more detailed assessment using STEEP, the results showed that, through a more rigorous operational plan and potentially by generating power from the excess hydraulic pressure from the surface supply, the energy use could actually be lowered to approximately 60% of the forecasted use (Figure 18). This is an example of how STEEP can be used to quickly identify anomalies that can lead the utility manager to find opportunities for generating savings from energy use.

■ Water System No. 2

Water System No. 2 is a good example of how STEEP can be used to alter a project at the transaction technical assistance stage to save on energy costs. Prior to the incorporated system upgrades, Water System No. 2 supplied less than half of the residents within its service area. The system is located in an area with significant elevation changes, where the water supply system network extends from elevations of approximately 100 meters above mean sea level to more than 220 meters above mean sea level. The proposed upgrades for Water System No. 2 include (i) a single well field, located at the lowest elevation; and (ii) a single pumping station to lift the water to a pressure sufficient to reach consumers located at the 220-meter elevation. The water pressure is then regulated to three pressure management zones through a series of pressure reducing valves.

While this system is simple to design, and most likely was the lowest capital cost option, it is inefficient in terms of energy use. It will also require a high level of skill and cost to operate and maintain. As an alternative, a system using separate pumping to the three zones individually was modeled (forecast and assessment shown in Figure 18) and became the basis for design alterations to the system, which then led to energy cost savings during its operation.

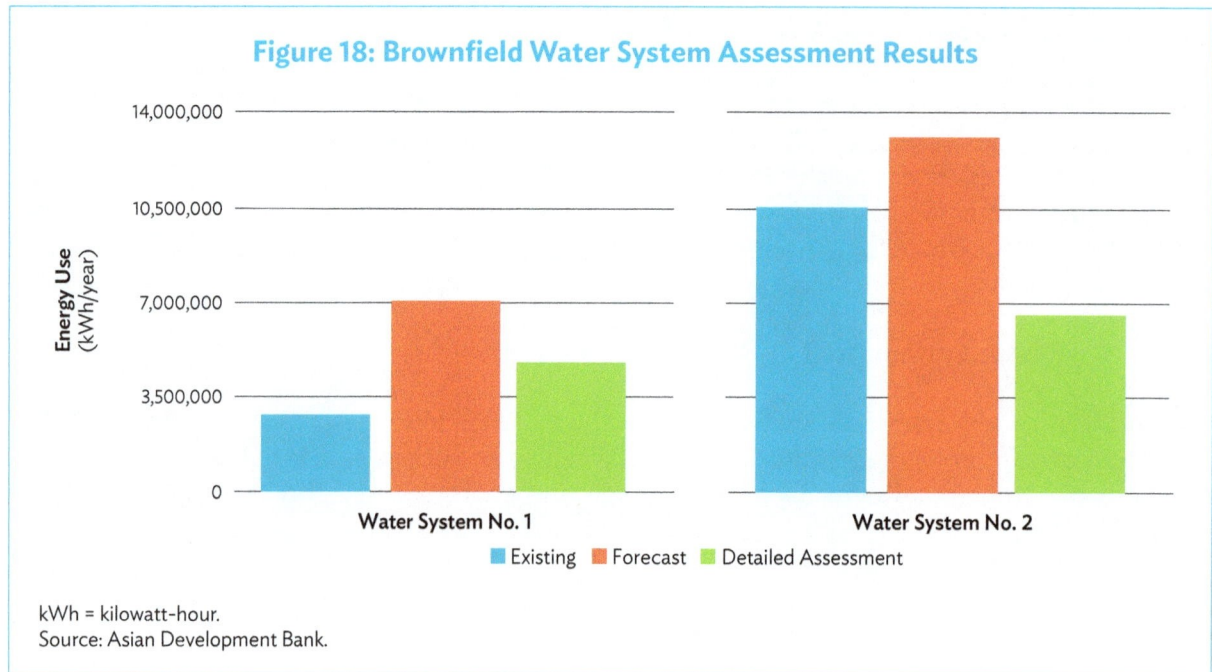

Figure 18: Brownfield Water System Assessment Results

kWh = kilowatt-hour.
Source: Asian Development Bank.

Pilot Case 3: Greenfield Wastewater Treatment Plant Example

In this case, the assessment scenario is for three recently constructed wastewater treatment plants. For these greenfield facilities, STEEP was used to assess and compare the energy use in the treatment facilities against the acceptable benchmarks and best practices. A more detailed analysis of the potential causes of energy inefficiency in the three facilities followed the initial assessment with STEEP.

As shown in Table 7, the plants utilize significantly more energy than the benchmark data and, in some cases, even more than double the specific energy use. A more detailed assessment for Plant No. 1 revealed that the aeration system, while designed with state-of-the-art equipment and controls, was installed incorrectly with the piping and valving. The system essentially did not adhere to best practices, with the aeration system constructed with the majority of the airflow volume being fed to the zones with the lowest air demand and the lowest airflow to the zones with the highest demand. The result was not only excessive energy use, but also poor wastewater treatment performance. An analysis that considered reconfiguring the system with only piping, valving, and control system changes resulted in a projected energy savings of more than 20%.

Tables 8–10 show the analysis inputs used for the three plants on the STEEP platform interface for data inputs.

Table 7: Operation Details of the Wastewater Treatment Plants

Plant	Process	Average Daily Flow (m^3/day)	Average Daily Electricity Use (kWh/day)
Plant No. 1	A_2O	50,000	12,000
Plant No. 2	SBR	80,000	18,000
Plant No. 3	Modified A_2O	270,000	38,000

A_2O = anaerobic/anoxic/oxic treatment process, kWh = kilowatt-hour, m^3= cubic meter, SBR = sequencing batch reactor.
Source: Asian Development Bank.

Table 8: Wastewater Plant No. 1 Data Inputs

Rapid Assessment Input Data-Wastewater (Required Data Inputs Marked *)

Rapid Assessment	Units	Definitions	Baseline Pre-Project Situation	Forecast Situation after Project Implementation	Comments
Number of Sewer Connections*	connections	Number of connections to the sewer system within the wastewater utility area	NA	NA	
Population of Service Area*	people	Number of inhabitants within the area of service managed by the wastewater utility	NA	NA	
Serviced (Connected) Population*	people	Number of people connected to the sewer and which wastewater reaches the treatment plant to be treated prior to discharge	184,500	NA	
Treated Wastewater Flow*	m^3	Total wastewater treated by the wastewater utility	16,605,092	NA	
BOD5 Removed*	ton	Total BOD5 removed by the wastewater utility	650	NA	
COD Removed*	ton	Total COD removed by the wastewater utility	1,519	NA	If no data are available, use 0.50 kg CO_2/kWh.
Specific Carbon Production*	kg CO_2/kWh	Specific CO_2 production per kWh for the electricity generation mix in the service area	0.50	NA	
Total Energy Consumed*	kWh	Total energy consumed for the entire wastewater based on the electricity bill during the entire assessment period	2,343,038	NA	
Renewable Energy Consumed	kWh	Total renewable energy consumed during the assessment period	NA	NA	
Energy Costs	$	Costs from electricity energy consumption for the entire wastewater utility based on the electricity bill during the entire assessment period	270,862	NA	
Chemical Costs	$	Costs from chemical consumption for the entire wastewater utility based on the chemical bill during the entire assessment period	18,000	NA	
Operating Costs	$	Total operation and maintenance net costs and internal human resources net costs (i.e., not including the capitalized cost of self-constructed assets) related to the wastewater within the service area managed by the utility during the entire assessment period	NA	NA	

continued on next page

Table 8 *continued*

Rapid Assessment	Units	Definitions	Baseline Pre-Project Situation	Forecast Situation after Project Implementation	Comments
Volume of Fuel Consumed	L	Fuel consumption in wastewater, for instance due to the use of on-site generators or devices that work on fuel (e.g., fuel for engines for pumps)	NA	NA	
Total Mass of Sludge Produced	dry ton	Total mass of sludge produced from the WWTP	1,666	NA	
Volatile Fraction of Sludge	%	Volatile fraction of sludge produced from the WWTP	NA	NA	
Total Wet Mass of Sludge Hauled to Disposal	wet ton	Total wet mass of sludge hauled to disposal	8,328	NA	
Distance to Sludge Disposal Site	km	Only if using truck transport to convey sludge to disposal site. If there is more than one disposal site, use an average value	27	NA	
Sludge Disposal Costs	$	Total yearly cost to dispose of sludge from the WWTP to its ultimate disposal site (includes hauling and tipping/disposal fees)	NA	NA	
Chemical Costs of Sludge Treatment	$	Costs from chemical consumption for the sludge treatment based on the chemical bill during the entire assessment period	14,342	NA	
Average Total Nitrogen at Discharge	mg/L	Concentration of total nitrogen in mg per liter of treated wastewater	NA	NA	
Annual Protein Consumption per Capita	kg/people/year	Preferably this value needs to be an actual measured value for your system. If not, use referential value from, eg, the FAO Statistics Division	NA	NA	
Biogas Produced	m³	Biogas produced by the wastewater utility during the evaluation period	NA	NA	
Collection Energy Consumed by the Collection System	kWh	Electric energy consumption for wastewater collection by the utility during the entire assessment period	NA	NA	
Collection Volume of Conveyed Wastewater	m³	Sum of the wastewater conveyed to the treatment plants by the utility during the entire assessment period	NA	NA	
Treatment Energy Consumed by WWTPs	kWh	Energy consumed during the assessment period by all urban wastewater treatments plant managed by the utility	2,343,038	NA	
Treatment Energy Consumed by Aeration Process	kWh	Energy consumed during the assessment period by the aeration process at all urban wastewater treatments plant managed by the utility	NA	NA	
Treatment Volume of Wastewater Treated	m³	Sum of the volume of wastewater treated by the wastewater treatment stage during the assessment period	16,605,092	NA	

$ = United States dollar, BOD5 = biological oxygen demand over 5 days, CO_2 = carbon dioxide, COD = chemical oxygen demand, FAO = Food and Agriculture Organization of the United Nations, kg = kilogram, km = kilometer, kWh = kilowatt-hour, L = liter, m³ = cubic meter, mg = milligram, NA = not applicable, WWTP = wastewater treatment plant.
Source: Asian Development Bank.

Table 9: Wastewater Plant No. 2 Data Inputs

Rapid Assessment Input Data – Wastewater (Required Data Inputs Marked *)

Rapid Assessment	Units	Definitions	Baseline Pre-Project Situation	Forecast Situation after Project Implementation	Comments
Number of Sewer Connections*	connections	Number of connections to the sewer system within the wastewater utility area	NA	NA	
Population of Service Area*	people	Number of inhabitants within the area of service managed by the wastewater utility	NA	NA	
Serviced (Connected) Population*	people	Number of people connected to the sewer and which wastewater reaches the treatment plant to be treated prior to discharge	232,200	NA	
Treated Wastewater Flow*	m^3	Total wastewater treated by the wastewater utility	26,839,440	NA	
BOD5 Removed*	ton	Total BOD5 removed by the wastewater utility	1,357	NA	
COD Removed*	ton	Total COD removed by the wastewater utility	3,185	NA	If no data are available, use 0.50 kg CO_2/kWh.
Specific Carbon Production*	kg CO_2/kWh	Specific CO_2 production per kWh for the electricity generation mix in the service area	0.50	NA	
Total Energy Consumed*	kWh	Total energy consumed for the entire wastewater based on the electricity bill during the entire assessment period	3,498,272	NA	
Renewable Energy Consumed	kWh	Total renewable energy consumed during the assessment period	NA	NA	
Energy Costs	$	Costs from electricity energy consumption for the entire wastewater utility based on the electricity bill during the entire assessment period	346,594	NA	
Chemical Costs	$	Costs from chemical consumption for the entire wastewater utility based on the chemical bill during the entire assessment period	79,846	NA	
Operating Costs	$	Total operation and maintenance net costs and internal human resources net costs (i.e., not including the capitalized cost of self-constructed assets) related to the wastewater within the service area managed by the utility during the entire assessment period	NA	NA	
Volume of Fuel Consumed	L	Fuel consumption in wastewater, for instance due to the use of on-site generators or devices that work on fuel (e.g., fuel for engines for pumps)	NA	NA	
Total Mass of Sludge Produced	dry ton	Total mass of sludge produced from the WWTP	NA	NA	
Volatile Fraction of Sludge	%	Volatile fraction of sludge produced from the WWTP	NA	NA	

continued on next page

Table 9 *continued*

	Rapid Assessment	Units	Definitions	Baseline Pre-Project Situation	Forecast Situation after Project Implementation	Comments
	Total Wet Mass of Sludge Hauled to Disposal	wet ton	Total wet mass of sludge hauled to disposal	NA	NA	
	Distance to Sludge Disposal Site	km	Only if using truck transport to convey sludge to disposal site. If there is more than one disposal site, use an average value	NA	NA	
	Sludge Disposal Costs	$	Total yearly cost to dispose of sludge from the WWTP to its ultimate disposal site (includes hauling and tipping/disposal fees)	NA	NA	
	Chemical Costs of Sludge Treatment	$	Costs from chemical consumption for the sludge treatment based on the chemical bill during the entire assessment period	17,832	NA	
	Average Total Nitrogen at Discharge	mg/L	Concentration of total nitrogen in mg per liter of treated wastewater	NA	NA	
	Annual Protein Consumption per Capita	kg/people/ year	Preferably this value needs to be an actual measured value for your system. If not, use referential value from, eg, the FAO Statistics Division	NA	NA	
	Biogas Produced	m³	Biogas produced by the wastewater utility during the evaluation period	NA	NA	
Collection	Energy Consumed by the Collection System	kWh	Electric energy consumption for wastewater collection by the utility during the entire assessment period	NA	NA	
	Volume of Conveyed Wastewater	m³	Sum of the wastewater conveyed to the treatment plants by the utility during the entire assessment period	NA	NA	
Treatment	Energy Consumed by WWTPs	kWh	Energy consumed during the assessment period by all urban wastewater treatments plant managed by the utility	3,498,272	NA	
	Energy Consumed by Aeration Process	kWh	Energy consumed during the assessment period by the aeration process at all urban wastewater treatments plant managed by the utility	NA	NA	
	Volume of Wastewater Treated	m³	Sum of the volume of wastewater treated by the wastewater treatment stage during the assessment period	26,839,440	NA	

$ = United States dollar, BOD5 = biological oxygen demand over 5 days, CO_2 = carbon dioxide, COD = chemical oxygen demand, FAO = Food and Agriculture Organization of the United Nations, kg = kilogram, km = kilometer, kWh = kilowatt-hour, L = liter, m³ = cubic meter, mg = milligram, NA = not applicable, WWTP = wastewater treatment plant.
Source: Asian Development Bank.

Table 10: Wastewater Plant No. 3 Data Inputs

Rapid Assessment Input Data-Wastewater (Required Data Inputs Marked *)

Rapid Assessment	Units	Definitions	Baseline Pre-Project Situation	Forecast Situation after Project Implementation	Comments
Number of Sewer Connections*	connections	Number of connections to the sewer system within the wastewater utility area	NA	NA	
Population of Service Area*	people	Number of inhabitants within the area of service managed by the wastewater utility	NA	NA	
Serviced (Connected) Population*	people	Number of people connected to the sewer and which wastewater reaches the treatment plant to be treated prior to discharge	2,391,750	NA	
Treated Wastewater Flow*	m³	Total wastewater treated by the wastewater utility	87,389,870	NA	
BOD5 Removed*	ton	Total BOD5 removed by the wastewater utility	4,970	NA	
COD Removed*	ton	Total COD removed by the wastewater utility	11,494	NA	If no data are available, use 0.50 kg CO_2/kWh.
Specific Carbon Production*	kg CO_2/kWh	Specific CO_2 production per kWh for the electricity generation mix in the service area	0.50	NA	
Total Energy Consumed*	kWh	Total energy consumed for the entire wastewater based on the electricity bill during the entire assessment period	7,482,839	NA	
Renewable Energy Consumed	kWh	Total renewable energy consumed during the assessment period	NA	NA	
Energy Costs	$	Costs from electricity energy consumption for the entire wastewater utility based on the electricity bill during the entire assessment period	743,669	NA	
Chemical Costs	$	Costs from chemical consumption for the entire wastewater utility based on the chemical bill during the entire assessment period	358,196	NA	
Operating Costs	$	Total operation and maintenance net costs and internal human resources net costs (i.e., not including the capitalized cost of self-constructed assets) related to the wastewater within the service area managed by the utility during the entire assessment period	NA	NA	
Volume of Fuel Consumed	L	Fuel consumption in wastewater, for instance due to the use of on-site generators or devices that work on fuel (e.g., fuel for engines for pumps)	NA	NA	
Total Mass of Sludge Produced	dry ton	Total mass of sludge produced from the WWTP	7,560	NA	
Volatile Fraction of Sludge	%	Volatile fraction of sludge produced from the WWTP	NA	NA	

continued on next page

Table 10 *continued*

	Rapid Assessment	Units	Definitions	Baseline Pre-Project Situation	Forecast Situation after Project Implementation	Comments
	Total Wet Mass of Sludge Hauled to Disposal	wet ton	Total wet mass of sludge hauled to disposal	18,900	NA	
	Distance to Sludge Disposal Site	km	Only if using truck transport to convey sludge to disposal site. If there is more than one disposal site, use an average value	6	NA	
	Sludge Disposal Costs	$	Total yearly cost to dispose of sludge from the WWTP to its ultimate disposal site (includes hauling and tipping/disposal fees)	71,244	NA	
	Chemical Costs of Sludge Treatment	$	Costs from chemical consumption for the sludge treatment based on the chemical bill during the entire assessment period	397,825	NA	
	Average Total Nitrogen at Discharge	mg/L	Concentration of total nitrogen in mg per liter of treated wastewater	NA	NA	
	Annual Protein Consumption per Capita	kg/people/year	Preferably this value needs to be an actual measured value for your system. If not, use referential value from, eg, the FAO Statistics Division	NA	NA	
	Biogas Produced	m^3	Biogas produced by the wastewater utility during the evaluation period	NA	NA	
Collection	Energy Consumed by the Collection System	kWh	Electric energy consumption for wastewater collection by the utility during the entire assessment period	NA	NA	
	Volume of Conveyed Wastewater	m^3	Sum of the wastewater conveyed to the treatment plants by the utility during the entire assessment period	NA	NA	
Treatment	Energy Consumed by WWTPs	kWh	Energy consumed during the assessment period by all urban wastewater treatments plant managed by the utility	7,482,839	NA	
	Energy Consumed by Aeration Process	kWh	Energy consumed during the assessment period by the aeration process at all urban wastewater treatments plant managed by the utility	NA	NA	
	Volume of Wastewater Treated	m^3	Sum of the volume of wastewater treated by the wastewater treatment stage during the assessment period	87,389,870	NA	

$ = United States dollar, BOD5 = biological oxygen demand over 5 days, CO_2 = carbon dioxide, COD = chemical oxygen demand, FAO = Food and Agriculture Organization of the United Nations, kg = kilogram, km = kilometer, kWh = kilowatt-hour, L = liter, m^3 = cubic meter, mg = milligram, NA = not applicable, WWTP = wastewater treatment plant.
Source: Asian Development Bank.

Aeration systems are typically the largest energy consumers in wastewater treatment plants. It is also the most difficult to efficiently control, especially if the focus is on treatment efficiency and not energy efficiency. Moreover, many wastewater treatment systems are over-aerated to assure better treatment, which results in excessive energy use. Figure 19 shows the results of this analysis.

Figure 19: Wastewater Example Project Assessment Results

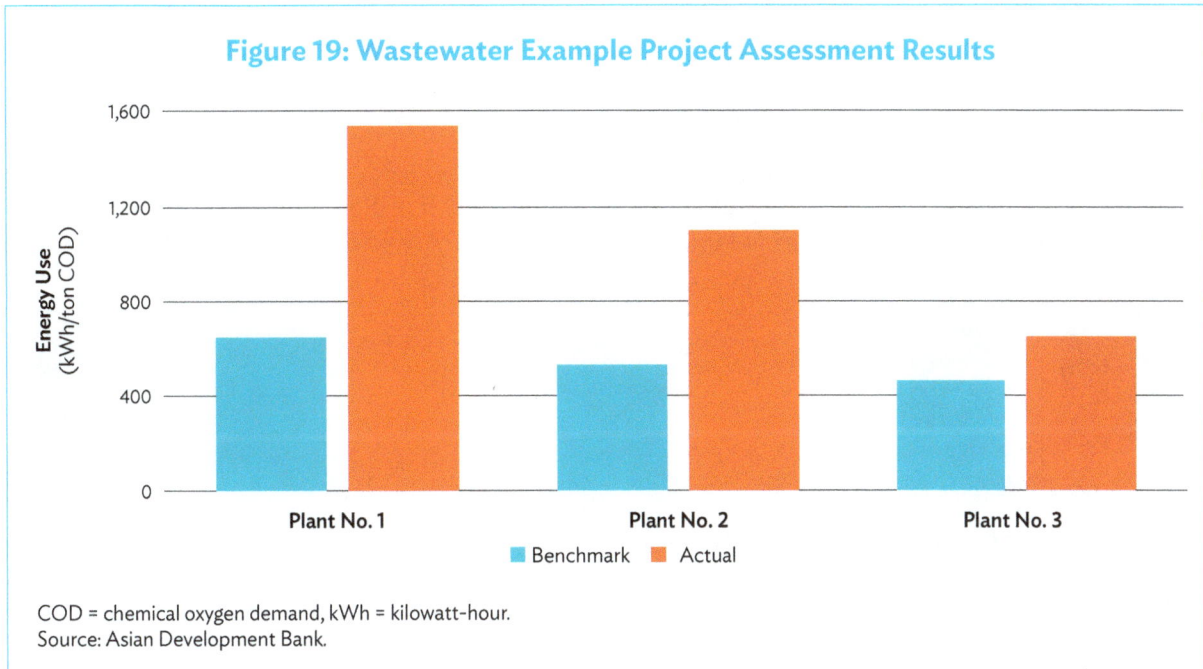

COD = chemical oxygen demand, kWh = kilowatt-hour.
Source: Asian Development Bank.

APPENDIXES

STEEP SAMPLE WORKSHEETS

1.   Project General Information Pages

Go to the Asian Development Bank (ADB) site, Vision of Livable Cities, to download the Toolkits: Screening Tool for Energy Evaluation of Projects (STEEP). https://www.livablecities.info/steep.

Back to Welcome Page	**ADB**	Screening Tool for Energy Evaluation in Projects (STEEP) A Practical Guide for ADB Staff Main	Back to Instructions

Please answer the questions below.

1. What system(s) are you evaluating?	**Select here**
2. Are there any existing systems?	**Yes**
2.a. If yes, what systems are existing?	*Both WS+WW*

WS = water supply, WW = wastewater.

Back to Welcome Page	**ADB**	Screening Tool for Energy Evaluation in Projects (STEEP) A Practical Guide for ADB Staff General Information	Back to Main	Back to Instructions

Instruction: Please fill-in information below.

Name of System:	**Sample**
Location:	**Location**

General Information	Units	Definitions	Baseline Pre-Project Situation	Forecast Situation After Project Implementation	Comments
Brief Description*	na	Provide general information about the system and context	Sample description	Sample description	
Start Date*	mm/dd/yyyy	Date when the assessment starts	01/01/17	01/01/22	
End Date*	mm/dd/yyyy	Date when the assessment ends	12/31/17	12/31/22	
Assessment Period*	days	Total number of days in which the assessment is based (ideally 365 days)	364	364	

2.   Water Supply Assessment Inputs

Rapid Assessment	Units	Definitions	Baseline Pre-Project Situation	Forecast Situation after Project Implementation	Comments
Number of Connections*	connections	Number of connections to the distribution system and receiving the service, within the area of service managed by the utility	3,978	11,951	
Population of Service Area*	people	Number of inhabitants, within the area of service managed by the utility	76,855	85,961	
Serviced (Connected) Population*	people	Number of inhabitants, within the area of service managed by the utility, which are connected to the distribution system and are receiving the service	28,529	85,961	
Total Water Produced*	m^3	Total water consumed or used in the system, including (i) authorized consumption and (b) water loss	951,132	2,377,830	
Authorized Consumption*	m^3	Sum of the volume of metered and nonmetered water that , during the assessment period, is taken by registered customers, water supplier, or others who are implicitly or explicitly authorized to do so by the water supplier, for residential, commercial, industrial, or public purposes (includes water exported)	615,273	1,786,995	
Specific Carbon Production*	kg CO_2/kWh	Specific CO_2 production per kWh for electricity generation mix in the service area	0.50	0.50	If data are not available, use 0.50 kg CO_2/kWh.

CO_2 = carbon dioxide, kg = kilogram, kWh = kilowatt-hour, m^3 = cubic meter.
Note: The actual tool would require more input data.

3.   Water Supply System Scorecard

Parameter	Baseline Project Situation	Forecast Situation after Project Implementation	Unit	KPI Parameters
Energy Use per Authorized Consumption	0.30	2.90	kWh/m³	<0.45 desirable; 0.70 marginal; >1.30 undesirable
Energy Use per Produced Flow	0.19	2.18	kWh/m³	<0.35 desirable; 0.45 marginal; >0.65 undesirable
Nonrevenue Water	35.31	24.85	%	<20 desirable; 35 marginal; >50 undesirable
Per Capita Consumption (daily)	91.59	75.99	L/c/d	<100 desirable; 150 marginal; >250 undesirable
CO_2 Emissions per Capita (service area)	1.20	30.18	kg CO_2/c/year	<5 desirable; 1 0 marginal; > 15 undesirable

Water—Energy Trajectory: Pre- and Post-Project

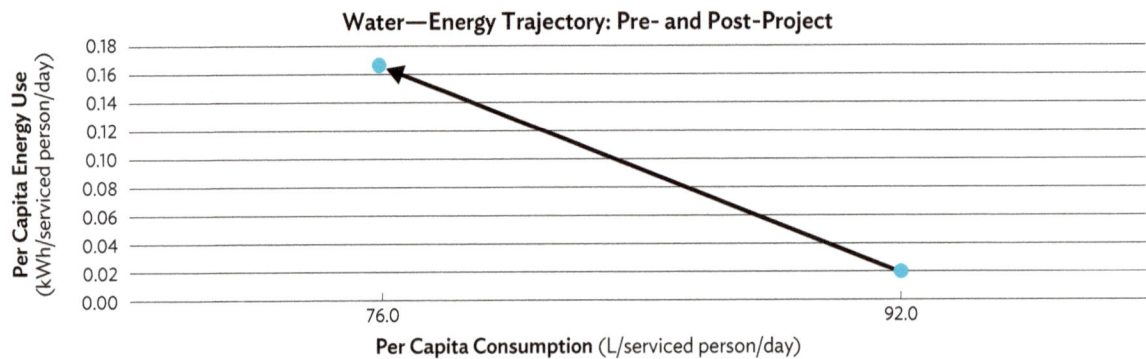

KPI = key performance indicator, kWh = kilowatt-hour, L = liter, L/c/d = liters per capita per day, m³ = cubic meter.
Note: The colors in the table are data-driven to depict level of outputs: green (desirable), light green (at a range between desirable and marginal), yellow (marginal), orange (at a range between marginal and undesirable), and red (undesirable).

4. Water System Assessment Output Graphs

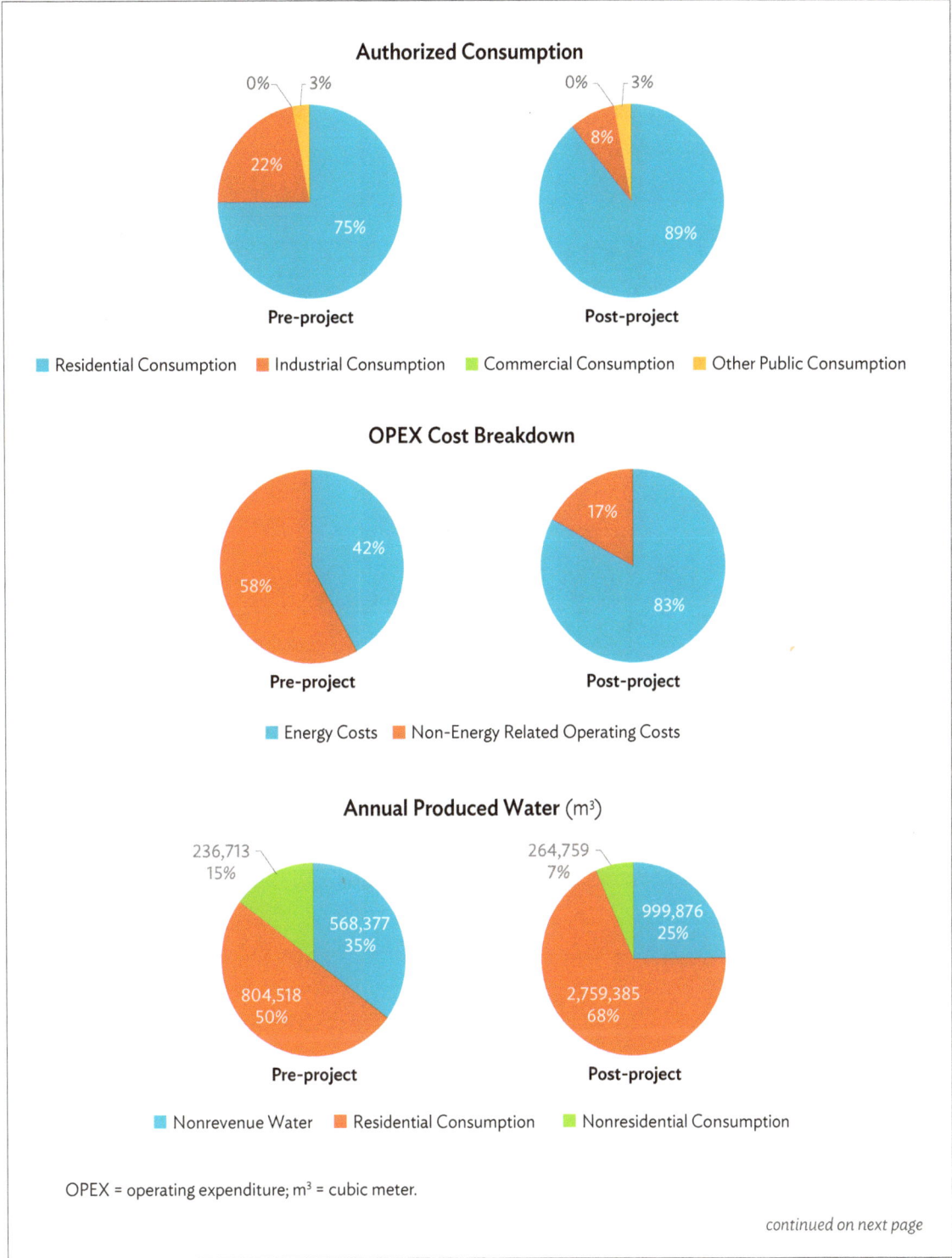

Authorized Consumption

0% 3%
22%
75%
Pre-project

0% 3%
8%
89%
Post-project

■ Residential Consumption ■ Industrial Consumption ■ Commercial Consumption ■ Other Public Consumption

OPEX Cost Breakdown

42%
58%
Pre-project

17%
83%
Post-project

■ Energy Costs ■ Non-Energy Related Operating Costs

Annual Produced Water (m³)

236,713
15%
568,377
35%
804,518
50%
Pre-project

264,759
7%
999,876
25%
2,759,385
68%
Post-project

■ Nonrevenue Water ■ Residential Consumption ■ Nonresidential Consumption

OPEX = operating expenditure; m³ = cubic meter.

continued on next page

Appendix 4 *continued*

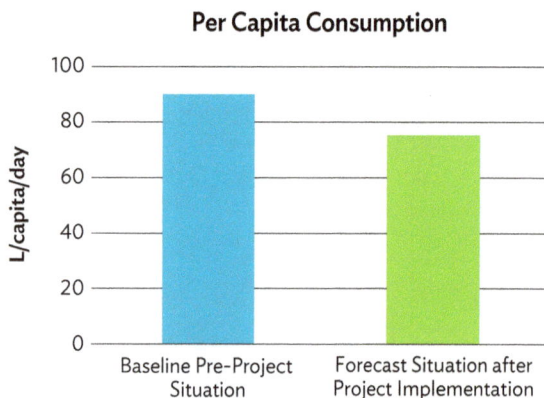

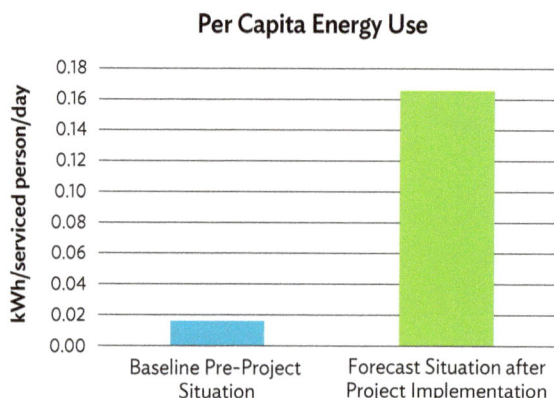

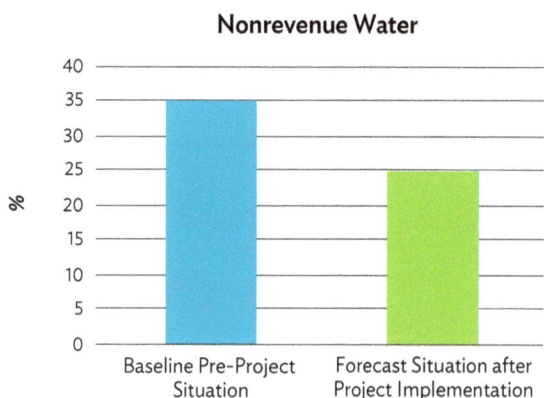

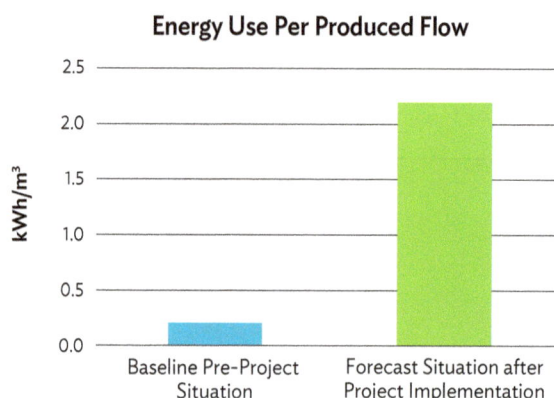

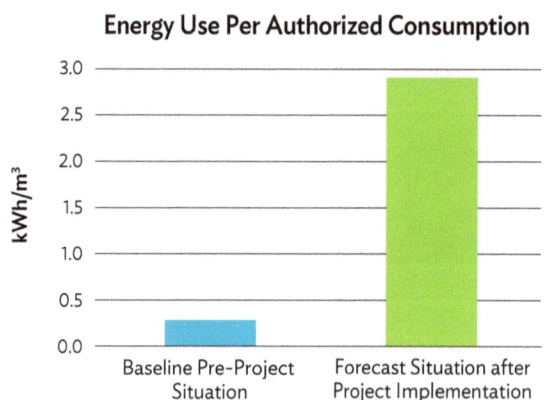

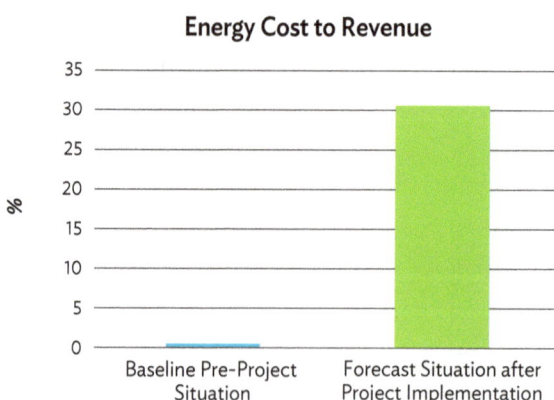

Per Capita Consumption

L/capita/day — Baseline Pre-Project Situation: ~90; Forecast Situation after Project Implementation: ~75

Per Capita Energy Use

kWh/serviced person/day — Baseline Pre-Project Situation: ~0.015; Forecast Situation after Project Implementation: ~0.165

Nonrevenue Water

% — Baseline Pre-Project Situation: ~35; Forecast Situation after Project Implementation: ~24.5

Energy Use Per Produced Flow

kWh/m³ — Baseline Pre-Project Situation: ~0.2; Forecast Situation after Project Implementation: ~2.2

Energy Use Per Authorized Consumption

kWh/m³ — Baseline Pre-Project Situation: ~0.27; Forecast Situation after Project Implementation: ~2.9

Energy Cost to Revenue

% — Baseline Pre-Project Situation: ~0.3; Forecast Situation after Project Implementation: ~30.5

kWh = kilowatt-hour, L = liter, m³ = cubic meter.
Source: Asian Development Bank.

5.   Wastewater Treatment System Assessment Inputs

Rapid Assessment	Units	Definitions	Baseline Pre-Project Situation	Forecast Situation after Project Implementation	Comments
Renewable Energy Consumed	kWh	Total renewable energy consumed during the assessment period	NA	NA	
Energy Costs	$	Costs from electricity energy consumption for the entire wastewater utility based on the electricity bill during the entire assessment period	401,276	320,451	
Chemical Costs	$	Costs from chemical consumption for the entire wastewater utility based on the chemical bill during the entire assessment period	16,000	16,800	
Operating Costs	$	Total operation and maintenance net costs and internal human resources net costs (i.e., not including the capitalized cost of self-constructed assets) related to the wastewater within the service area managed by the utility during the entire assessment period	NA	NA	
Volume of Fuel Consumed	L	Fuel consumption in wastewater, for instance due to the use of on-site generators or devices that work on fuel (e.g., fuel for engines for pumps)	NA	NA	
Total Mass of Sludge Produced	dry tons	Total mass of sludge produced from the WWTP	1,481	1,360	
Volatile Fraction of Sludge	%	Volatile fraction of sludge produced from the WWTP	NA	NA	
Total Wet Mass of Sludge Hauled to Disposal	wet tons	Total wet mass of sludge hauled to disposal	7,403	6,800	
Distance to Sludge Disposal Site	km	Only if using truck transport to convey sludge to disposal site. If there is more than one disposal site, use an average value.	24	24	

$ = United States dollar, km = kilometer, kWh = kilowatt-hour, L = liter, NA = not applicable, WWTP = wastewater treatment plant.
Note: The actual tool would require more input data.
Source: Asian Development Bank.

6.   Wastewater Treatment System Scorecard

Parameter	Baseline Project Situation	Forecast Situation after Project Implementation	Unit	KPI Parameters
Energy Use per Ton of BOD5 Removal	6,010	4,571	kWh/ton BOD5 removed	<1,200 desirable; 1,500 marginal; >1,800 undesirable
Energy Use per Ton of COD Removal	2,570	1,955	kWh/ton COD removed	<800 desirable; 1,000 marginal; >1,200 undesirable
Energy Use per Treated Wastewater Flow	0.24	0.17	kWh/m³	<0.25 desirable; 0.5 marginal; >0.7 undesirable

Wastewater—Energy Trajectory: Pre- and Post-Project

Per Capita Energy Use (kWh/serviced person/day) vs Per Capita Flow (L/serviced person/day)

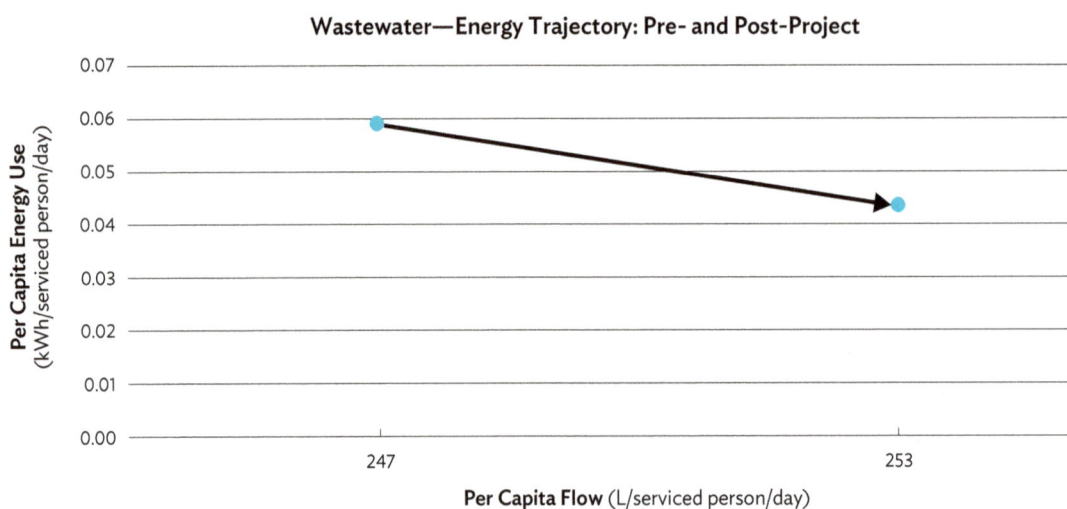

BOD5 = biological oxygen demand over 5 days, COD = chemical oxygen demand, kWh = kilowatt-hour, L = liter, m³ = cubic meter.
Source: Asian Development Bank.

7.   Wastewater Treatment System Assessment Output Graphs

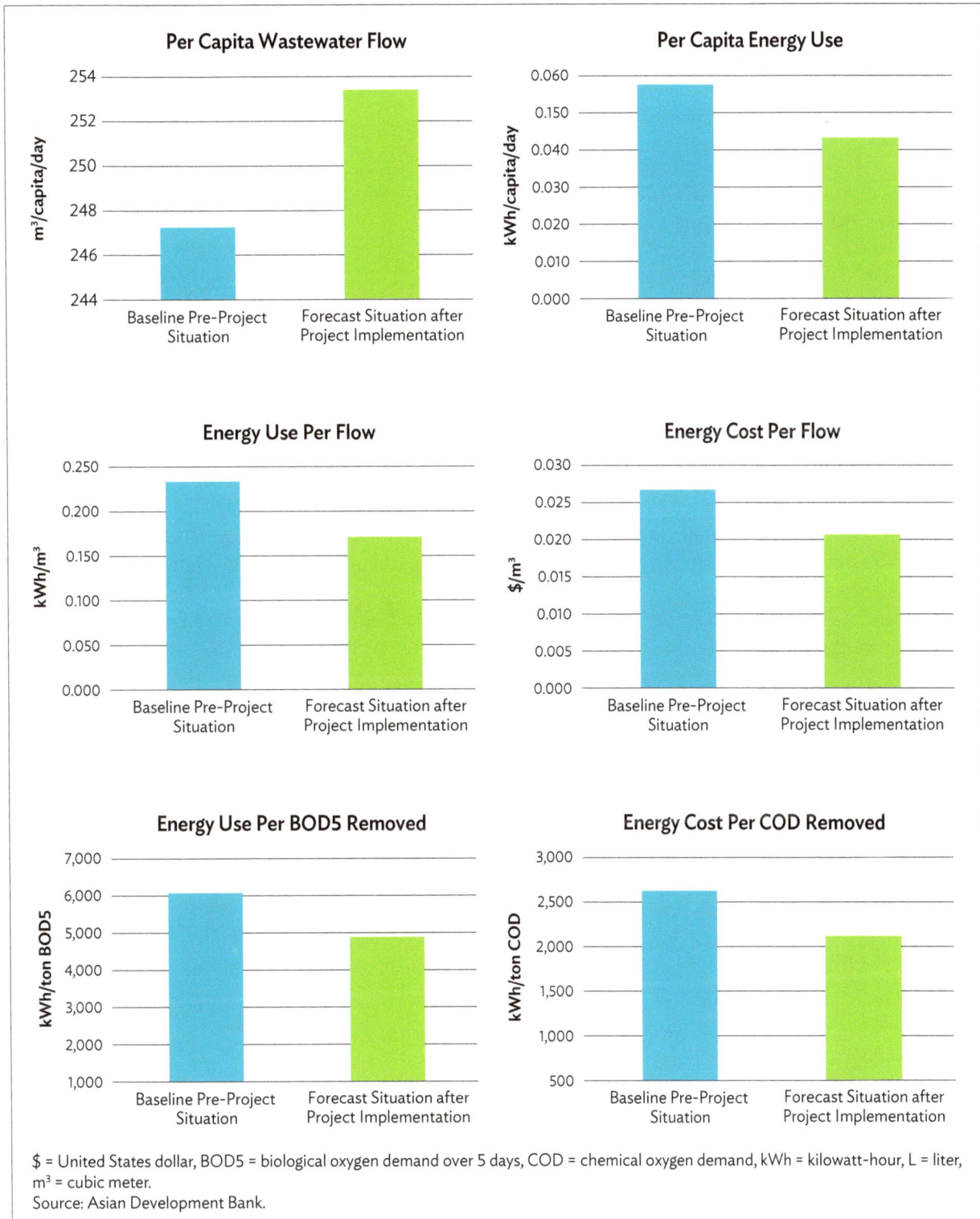

Per Capita Wastewater Flow — Baseline Pre-Project Situation ~247.3; Forecast Situation after Project Implementation ~253.5 (m^3/capita/day)

Per Capita Energy Use — Baseline ~0.058; Forecast ~0.043 (kWh/capita/day)

Energy Use Per Flow — Baseline ~0.235; Forecast ~0.172 (kWh/m^3)

Energy Cost Per Flow — Baseline ~0.0267; Forecast ~0.0207 ($/m^3$)

Energy Use Per BOD5 Removed — Baseline ~6,075; Forecast ~4,900 (kWh/ton BOD5)

Energy Cost Per COD Removed — Baseline ~2,625; Forecast ~2,125 (kWh/ton COD)

$ = United States dollar, BOD5 = biological oxygen demand over 5 days, COD = chemical oxygen demand, kWh = kilowatt-hour, L = liter, m^3 = cubic meter.
Source: Asian Development Bank.

REFERENCES

Asian Development Bank (ADB). 2016. *The Asian Development Bank and the Climate Investment Funds: Country Fact Sheets.* Manila.

————. 2017. Energy Utilization Screening Methodology for ADB Municipal Water Projects: A Practical Guide for ADB Staff. Unpublished.

K. Bijl, ed. 2015. *Innovative Energy Recovery Strategies in the Urban Water Cycle.* Final Report Innovative Energy Recoveries Strategy (INNERS) Project. Zwolle.

J. Chen et al. 2013. A Novel Vertical Axis Water Turbine for Power Generation from Water Pipelines. *Energy.* 54. pp. 184–193.

Enerwater. 2015. Standard Method and Online Tool for Assessing and Improving the Energy Efficiency of Wastewater Treatment Plants: Deliverable 2.1 Study of Published Energy Data. 30 September.

G. Hayward. 2018. City of Gresham: Upgrading a Wastewater Treatment Plant to be Energy Net Zero. Center for Sustainable Infrastructure. Gresham, Oregon. August.

Singapore Public Utilities Board. 2013. *Towards Energy Self-Sufficient Water Reclamation Plants: A R&D Literature Review on Used Water Technologies.* Singapore.

WaterWorld. 2012. Water Utility Efficiency Priorities: What Are They?

www.ingramcontent.com/pod-product-compliance
Lightning Source LLC
Chambersburg PA
CBHW050056220326
41599CB00045B/7434